Lincoln's Last Card

Landmark Presidential Decisions

Series Editor
Michael Nelson

Advisory Board
Meena Bose
Brendan J. Doherty
Richard J. Ellis
Lori Cox Han
James Oakes
Barbara A. Perry
Andrew Rudalevige

Lincoln's Last Card

The Emancipation Proclamation as a Case of Command

Richard J. Ellis

University Press of Kansas

© 2025 by the University Press of Kansas
All rights reserved

Published by the University Press of Kansas (Lawrence, Kansas 66045), which was organized by the Kansas Board of Regents and is operated and funded by Emporia State University, Fort Hays State University, Kansas State University, Pittsburg State University, the University of Kansas, and Wichita State University.

Library of Congress Cataloging-in-Publication Data

Names: Ellis, Richard (Richard J.), author.
Title: Lincoln's last card : the Emancipation Proclamation as a case of command / Richard J. Ellis.
Description: Lawrence, Kansas : University Press of Kansas, 2025. | Series: Landmark presidential decisions | Includes bibliographical references and index.
Identifiers: LCCN 2024028935 (print) | LCCN 2024028936 (ebook) | ISBN 9780700638123 (cloth) | ISBN 9780700638130 (paperback) | ISBN 9780700638147 (ebook)
Subjects: LCSH: United States. President (1861–1865 : Lincoln). Emancipation Proclamation. | Lincoln, Abraham, 1809–1865. | Enslaved persons—Emancipation—United States. | Political leadership—United States. | Executive power—United States. | Presidents—United States—Biography. | United States—Politics and government—1861–1865. | BISAC: HISTORY / United States / Civil War Period (1850–1877) | SOCIAL SCIENCE / Slavery
Classification: LCC E453 .E955 2025 (print) | LCC E453 (ebook) | DDC 973.7/14—dc23/eng/20241029
LC record available at https://lccn.loc.gov/2024028935.
LC ebook record available at https://lccn.loc.gov/2024028936.

British Library Cataloguing-in-Publication Data is available.

For my students and colleagues at Willamette University

CONTENTS

Foreword by James Oakes   ix

Preface and Acknowledgments   xi

Introduction: Lincoln as Leader, Neustadt as Teacher   1

Chapter 1. A Command Aborted: The First Proclamation of Emancipation   7

Chapter 2. A Failure to Persuade: Lincoln's Plan for Compensated Emancipation in the Border States   19

Chapter 3. A Painful Last Resort: Lincoln's Decision to Emancipate   28

Chapter 4. A Failure to Persuade (Again): Lincoln's Colonization Plan   33

Chapter 5. "The Time Has Come Now": The Preliminary Proclamation   40

Chapter 6. The Cost of Command: The Fall Elections   50

Chapter 7. On Deaf Ears: Lincoln's Final "Olive Branch"   61

Chapter 8. "An Act of Justice": The Final Proclamation   69

Chapter 9. A Less than Conclusive Order   81

Conclusion: Lessons and Legacies   95

Notes   103

Bibliographic Essay   133

Index   145

FOREWORD

The competing myths about Abraham Lincoln and the Emancipation Proclamation never seem to die. He was either the Great Emancipator who freed all the slaves with the stroke of his pen or he was the reluctant emancipator, held back by his racism, "forced into glory" by others, including the slaves themselves. In *Lincoln's Last Card,* his brief but compelling account, Richard Ellis takes aim at both of these myths. They are too simple, Ellis notes. They don't take into account the complicated origins of the Emancipation Proclamation, and they most certainly don't make sense of Lincoln's own view of its very real limitations.

For Professor Ellis, Lincoln exemplifies not the strength but the weakness of the American presidency. Drawing on the classic scholarship of Richard Neustadt, Ellis argues that Lincoln turned to the proclamation only as a last resort, having failed in his primary goal of getting the four border slave states to adopt his plan for gradual abolition. This is an interpretation that will be familiar to all scholars of Lincoln and emancipation, and I must say I'm not fully persuaded. Military emancipation began months before Lincoln started pressuring the border states, and the Emancipation Proclamation gave Lincoln extra leverage to put still more pressure on those states.

Nevertheless, Ellis is surely right that Lincoln's "decision" to issue the Proclamation was driven by forces beyond his control, above all by the Second Confiscation Act passed by Congress in July 1862. In announcing the Proclamation two months after signing the act into law, Lincoln was merely complying with congressional mandate. Had he failed to do so, Ellis points out, Lincoln would have provoked a rebellion within his own party.

Having issued the Proclamation on January 1, 1863, Lincoln was surprisingly skeptical that it would have the dramatic impact predicted by its most ardent supporters or, for that matter, its most scandalized critics. As Ellis demonstrates, Lincoln clearly understood what the Proclamation could and could not do. Above all, declaring universal emancipation did not make emancipation universal.

This is not to say, however, that the Emancipation Proclamation was a dead letter. On the contrary, Ellis points out that it was part of a larger effort to secure the political support and the military victories that made genuinely universal abolition possible by means of a Thirteenth Amendment to the Constitution. Perhaps more than anything else, the Emancipation Proclamation prepared the northern people to accept the amendment as a necessary accompaniment to Union military victory. This, surely, demonstrates the aptness of Neustadt's central point, that the power of the presidency is the power to persuade.

I doubt that we will ever be able to extinguish the competing myths about Lincoln and emancipation. But for anyone with an open mind, ready to accept complexity and nuance instead of mythology, there's no better place to start than with *Lincoln's Last Card*.

James Oakes
City University of New York Graduate Center

PREFACE AND ACKNOWLEDGMENTS

Lincoln got me my first job—or so I like to think. At least, I can say with certainty that the presentation that I gave those many years ago on how Lincoln used his cabinet members as lightning rods to deflect blame for unpopular policies didn't cost me the job. There weren't then and there aren't now a lot of freshly minted PhDs in political science who would think it a good idea to give their job talk on something as unquantifiable as Lincoln's leadership. Fortunately, I was lucky enough to give that talk to what may have been the one political science department in the country where that was not disqualifying. I am even more fortunate that after more than three decades teaching at Willamette University, I was afforded the opportunity to return to Lincoln. For that (and for much else) I thank Mike Nelson. When Mike approached me about writing on a landmark presidential decision for his new book series, my mind immediately gravitated to Lincoln. And from there it was only a short step to the Emancipation Proclamation. After all, what could be a more landmark presidential decision than the destruction of slavery, America's putative "original sin"?

We are accustomed to thinking about Lincoln through the prism of presidential greatness. He has finished atop virtually every ranking of presidential greatness that has been conducted over the last half century. Even President Donald Trump conceded that Honest Abe Lincoln was "tough to beat" in the greatness department. This is the Lincoln familiar to us as the "master politician" (Richard Current), the "political genius" (Doris Kearns Goodwin), and the "eloquent president" (Ronald White). My own earlier work on Lincoln was infused with a similarly deep admiration for Lincoln's political sagacity. But the more I read about Lincoln and the Emancipation Proclamation, the more I came to wonder whether mastery was the wrong way to think about Lincoln's presidential leadership. Instead, I began to ask whether it might be better to think about Lincoln's decision-making less in terms of presidential greatness than of presidential weakness. That thought led me back to Richard Neustadt's classic text *Presidential Power: The Politics of Leadership*, which is erected upon the premise of presidential weakness.

As a graduate student in the 1980s I, along with seemingly every other student of American politics, read Neustadt. I admit that the book didn't do a lot for me back then, and I had a hard time seeing what all the fuss was about. Ronald Reagan's presidency, which was upending the entrenched New Deal regime, didn't seem particularly weak. I was quick to dismiss the book as dated. After all, the "three cases of command" that open the book are drawn from the Truman presidency and Eisenhower's first term, well before I was even born and, more important, before the rise of what many observers had taken to calling the "imperial presidency." I suppose I was wary, too, of the book's Machiavellian orientation. Presidents seemed to have more than enough power, and I didn't see why political scientists should dedicate themselves to helping presidents accumulate still more power. I was also skeptical of Neustadt's book because I viewed it as a cornerstone of the discipline's concerted effort to leave behind the so-called traditional presidencies and focus instead almost exclusively on "the modern presidency" that supposedly began with FDR. One sign of how little I rated Neustadt's classic book is that during my first decade teaching the presidency at Willamette, I routinely left it off of the course syllabus.

I started to have second thoughts about the wisdom of snubbing Neustadt after an unfortunate incident involving one of my finest students, Dustin Buehler. A finalist for the prestigious Truman Scholarship, Dustin drew a Regional Review Panel that included a prominent presidency scholar. Observing that Dustin had taken my presidency class, the distinguished panelist lobbed what I am sure he thought was a softball question: What do you think of Neustadt's approach to the presidency? Poor Dustin had to confess that he'd never actually read Neustadt, an admission that was obviously an indictment of his misguided teacher and not of him but nonetheless was hardly the sort of answer calculated to help him secure a highly competitive fellowship worth many thousands of dollars—although a couple years later Dustin did secure an even more amazing if less lucrative honor by breaking the Guinness World Record for the longest lecture, after talking for nearly fifty-two consecutive hours about the history of the American presidency.

Did my decision not to grapple more seriously with Neustadt cost a dear student $30,000? Maybe not. But the thought nagged at me. So, the next time I taught the class, Neustadt was in. That meant I needed to go back and read him again, more carefully this time. To my surprise, the book spoke to me in ways that it hadn't before. It possessed depths that my younger self had never fully fathomed. To borrow from Mark Twain, the older I got, the smarter Neustadt apparently got. My hope is that this short book will help give students a better appreciation for Neustadt's enduring relevance than I had as a student.

In thinking about the relevance of Neustadt's work in understanding Lincoln's leadership and especially his most famous unilateral directive, I have been helped enormously by the rich body of scholarship that has grown up in the last several decades on the unilateral executive. The work of Doug Kriner and Dino Christenson as well as Andrew Rudalevige has been particularly invaluable. This book would also obviously not have been possible without the pathbreaking and meticulous scholarship of so many great Lincoln scholars. Michael Burlingame, Eric Foner, Allen Guelzo, William Harris, Louis Masur, Mark Neeley, and James Oakes are among the historians who have profoundly shaped my understanding of Lincoln and the Emancipation Proclamation. Reading their work—and the work of so many other fine historians—was a joy and an inspiration.

I owe a special debt of gratitude to the readers for the University Press of Kansas, Lori Cox Han and James Read, as well as to others who kindly read and critically commented on the manuscript, especially Louis Masur and Kegan Rascoe. I also want to thank the many folks at the University Press of Kansas who helped to bring to fruition this book, my seventh with the press. That I keep coming back to UPK is a sign of how much I value the incredible work that they do. No author could ask for a better publisher.

Finally, I am profoundly grateful for the many colleagues and students at Willamette University who have done so much for so long to help me thrive as a scholar and a teacher. This book is for all of them—for their small kindnesses and generous support, their wise counsel and challenging questions, and, most of all, for their abiding faith in the importance of a liberal arts education.

Lincoln's Last Card

INTRODUCTION: LINCOLN AS LEADER, NEUSTADT AS TEACHER

"Presidential *power* is the power to persuade" remains the most quoted sentence in the most widely read book ever written about the American presidency.[1] Published in the year of John F. Kennedy's election, Richard Neustadt's *Presidential Power* has framed the way political scientists teach the modern presidency for more than six decades. For all its influence, however, the book has had surprisingly little impact on the way we study and think about nineteenth and early twentieth century presidencies. And those "premodern" presidencies have had almost no effect on how we evaluate Neustadt's concepts.

Part of this may be Neustadt's own doing. The book's opening pages stress the difference in kind between the "power problems" inherent in "mid-century conditions," which afflicted the likes of Harry Truman and Dwight Eisenhower, and the conditions governing the way power was acquired and deployed during the time of a Grover Cleveland or James Polk.[2] The way power was used in these bygone times, according to Neustadt, was too different to be relevant to the experience of contemporary presidents who face "emergencies in policies" on a routine basis. Admittedly, Neustadt allowed that Abraham Lincoln, "plagued by Radicals and shunned by Democrats" in the midst of the cataclysmic Civil War, was an exception, "much closer to us in condition than in time." But the central thrust of Neustadt's teaching was that if we want to understand presidential power in the present and the future, we are better off leaving the distant past behind and to focus our attention instead on "modern presidents at work in modern government."[3]

My contention is that Neustadt sold himself and political science short and that many of his core insights and arguments have as much to teach us about so-called traditional presidents as modern ones. What Neustadt identifies as "the essence of the problem now before us"—that constitutional "'powers' are no guarantee of power"—was a fundamental problem facing presidents in the nineteenth century as well. These chief executives, too, found formal "powers" inadequate to meet the demands placed upon them and command insufficient for obtaining the results they desired. If the "underlying theme" of *Presidential Power* was "presidential weakness," that theme plays at least as well in the nineteenth century.[4]

To illustrate that weakness, Neustadt begins his book, paradoxically, with "three cases of command": Truman's removal of General Douglas MacArthur in 1951 for insubordination, Truman's nationalizing of the steel industry in 1952, and Eisenhower's dispatch of troops to Little Rock in 1954 to enforce the Supreme Court's school desegregation ruling. At first glance, each of these cases of command seems to belie the idea of weakness or the centrality of persuasion since in each case the president commanded and others obeyed. The general was removed, the steel mills were placed under government control, and the children were escorted safely to school. But Neustadt suggests that the appearance of presidential success is misleading because "in each case, the decisive order was a painful last resort, a forced response to the exhaustion of all other remedies, suggestive less of mastery than failure—the failure of attempts to gain an end by softer means."[5]

In Eisenhower's case, Neustadt notes, "there were few things he wanted *less* than federal troops enforcing the desegregation of a Southern school." Neustadt also shows that MacArthur's firing was "remarkably long delayed" and that Truman had repeatedly "tried to patch the damage [and] bridge the differences" rather than dismiss the popular general. In the case of the steel mills, the "drastic act" of seizure was only seriously considered after the Truman administration had repeatedly failed to negotiate a settlement between capital and labor that would achieve the steel production and price controls that Truman believed were necessary for the war effort in Korea. In each case, the resort to command was a consequence of the failure to persuade.[6]

A crucial corollary to Neustadt's argument is the limits on the president's power to persuade. That is why virtually "every major illustration" in Neustadt's book was "in some sense the story of a failure."[7] A central finding of political science research on the presidency, most associated with the work of George Edwards, is that presidents are rarely able to persuade others—whether in the mass public or the Washington community—to change their opinions. Their appeals, as Edwards shows in numerous studies of modern presidents, generally fall "on deaf ears."[8] At one level, Edwards's empirical work might seem to challenge Neustadt's precept that presidential power is the power to persuade, but in a more fundamental sense his findings underscore Neustadt's central insight about the weakness of the presidency.

Neustadt also draws attention to the ways that each of these commands, while a last resort, were ultimately "not 'last' at all." Eisenhower's order to deploy troops to Little Rock "bought time," but in the final analysis it "solved no desegregation problems, not even the local ones at Central High School." In firing MacArthur, Truman "did not end MacArthur's challenge to Administration policy"; that threat receded only after "the Senate inquiry that followed his removal—and by the start of truce talks in Korea." Truman's order to seize the steel mills was promptly nullified by the Supreme Court, but even had it not been overturned, the effectiveness of his directive in achieving his goals would still have been dependent on a settlement between unions and the steel companies. The order may have enhanced the president's bargaining position, but he "had no power—and seizure gave him none—to gain his ends by fiat." In the end, in short, "these 'last' resorts [were] less than conclusive."[9]

Finally, Neustadt underscores that command is "costly" and "rarely comes at bargain rates." Of course, the costs incurred by command must be weighed against the cost of "continuing inaction." Neustadt's point is not that presidents should avoid commands, but that they "turn out to share the character of all the softer measures they replace. They turn out to be incidents in a persuasive process where someone lacking absolute control seeks to get something done through others who have power to resist." When all is said and done, "Command is but a method of persuasion, not a substitute."[10]

Another important corollary to Neustadt's argument is provided by political scientists Dino Christenson and Douglas Kriner, who highlight the ways that presidents, even when acting unilaterally, are attuned to public opinion. Unilateral executive action is rarely "imperial" let alone dictatorial but remains constrained by the power of other political actors, at both the state and federal level, "to mobilize the public and bring popular pressure to bear on the White House." Not all presidential commands end up being popular, but successful presidents rarely act unilaterally on important issues without weighing how the command will be received by other political actors whose response will be crucial to "whether the public rallies behind unilateral action or mobilizes against it."[11]

In this book, I employ these core insights to reexamine what is perhaps the most celebrated case of command in the history of the American presidency: Lincoln's Emancipation Proclamation. My aim in doing so is both to illustrate the power of Neustadt's political science and to illuminate the constraints on and limits of Lincoln's leadership.

Viewing Lincoln's famous edict through the lens of Neustadt's political science highlights several aspects of Lincoln's proclamation that are not always adequately appreciated. Chief among these is that the proclamation was a "painful last resort," which Lincoln turned to only after he had repeatedly failed to persuade others to support his preferred plan of gradual, compensated emancipation, paired if possible with some level of voluntary emigration of freed slaves. Lincoln conceded as much when he confessed to an ally that the preliminary Emancipation Proclamation that he signed on September 22, 1862, and published to the nation the following day, was "my last card."[12]

In addition, Neustadt's perspective, together with the work of Christenson and Kriner, draws our attention to the ways that even after Lincoln determined he had no choice but to play that final card, several more months elapsed—and more, mostly failed, attempts at persuasion—before he decided he could safely play it. Lincoln understood that it would do him little good to issue a proclamation that lacked adequate popular support. Even after issuing the preliminary proclamation, Lincoln continued to strive, with uneven success at best, to make the order palatable to Northern Whites before issuing the final Emancipation Proclamation on January 1, 1863.

That we are ill prepared to think about Lincoln in terms of the failure to persuade is in part because we know that no other president had Lincoln's way with words. No presidential speech before or since can match the economy and power of the Gettysburg Address, from its famous opening clause ("Four score and seven years ago . . .") to its stirring finale (". . . that government of the people, by the people, for the people, shall not perish from the Earth."). His most well-known lines are etched in our cultural consciousness. Every one of us recognizes "with malice toward none, with charity for all," the opening clause of the final sentence of his second Inaugural Address, still generally considered the greatest inaugural address ever written. If any president should possess the power to persuade, it is Lincoln.

Telling the story of the Emancipation Proclamation as a tale of presidential weakness and failure to persuade is not to gainsay the document's historical importance or to minimize Lincoln's achievements as president. Indeed, viewing Lincoln's leadership through Neustadt's frame of reference can lead us to a more realistic and robust view of Lincoln's accomplishments as a leader and thereby help to inoculate us against a naïve cynicism or misguided presentism that dismisses Lincoln without reckoning with the constraints on his leadership.

At the time Lincoln issued the Emancipation Proclamation, many proslavery advocates accused the president of being a dictator and lambasted the "imperial pretension" of his directive. Many on the antislavery side, on the other hand, lamented how long it took Lincoln to get around to issuing the proclamation. "Why, having the war power in his hands, he did not proclaim emancipation at the beginning," predicted one abolitionist, will be the question that will "perplex the future historian." A century later, the writer Julius Lester echoed the same point: "How come it took him two whole years to free the slaves? His pen was sitting on his desk the whole time." Each of these criticisms suffer from the same mistake, reliant as they are on what Christenson and Kriner call the "myth of the imperial presidency."[13]

For all of his many failures to persuade, Lincoln understood Neustadt far better than many of his critics. Lincoln intuited not only how perilous reliance on president command would be but also how limited a proclamation was as an answer to the problem of race in the United States. Declaring slaves free, Lincoln well knew, would not make them free let alone equal citizens.

CHAPTER 1

A Command Aborted

The First Proclamation of Emancipation

"Their slaves, if any they have, are hereby declared free men." The words struck the country "like a thunder clap in a clear sky." The nation's first proclamation of emancipation applied to every slaveholder in Missouri found to have taken "an active part" in the fight against the Union Army. Those who had labored for decades to put an end to slavery in the United States hailed the directive for finally, after four months of fighting, transforming the bloody grind of civil war into a righteous battle against slavery. But it was not only abolitionists who praised the proclamation. Newspapers across the North, of nearly every political stripe, commended it. According to Iowa senator Joseph Grimes, "Everybody of every sect, party, sex, and color approves it." Even Lincoln's secretary of war telegraphed his congratulations. One person who did not approve of the order, however, was the president of the United States.[1]

Dated August 30, 1861, the proclamation came from the pen of General John C. Frémont, whom Lincoln had appointed as the commander of the Department of the West at the beginning of July. Frémont was a national celebrity and a politically well-connected one to boot. He had made his name as an explorer of the American West and parlayed that fame and his antislavery principles into being chosen, in 1856, as the first presidential nominee of the fledgling Republican Party. Six years before that he had been selected as California's first US senator, as a Democrat. Frémont had powerful political allies: he was married to the formidable daughter of Missouri's celebrated US senator Thomas Hart Benton, and became close friends with the Blairs, border state powerbrokers par excellence. Indeed, it was the lobbying of Lincoln's postmaster general Montgomery Blair and his brother, Missouri congressman Frank Blair, that persuaded Lincoln to appoint Frémont.[2]

The Department of the West covered a huge swath of territory stretching all the way to the Rockies, but it was headquartered in St. Louis.[3] Lincoln made clear that Frémont's main objective was to "clear the rebels" from Missouri, a crucial border state that Lincoln was determined to keep in the Union.[4] This was no easy task in a state in which political conflict had given way to "open warfare" between armed secessionists and unionists. Distrust of Lincoln and his administration ran deep in Missouri, where Lincoln had finished a distant fourth in the 1860 presidential election, garnering only 10 percent of the vote. The state's newly elected Democratic governor, Claiborne Jackson, favored secession, the state legislature was "dominated by southern rights men," and proslavery sentiment across the state ran strong, particularly outside St. Louis. Although Governor Jackson had failed to secure control of the large federal arsenal in St. Louis—the largest of any slave state—he had "absolute power over the state militia" and the financial backing of both the state legislature and "the state's mostly pro-Confederate bankers," as well as armed support from the Confederate government.[5]

Shortly before Frémont's belated arrival in St. Louis on July 25, a convention of dubious legality convened and dissolved the state legislature, purged all state officeholders, and created a new provisional government until new elections could be held in November.[6] The gravity of the situation was underscored by the newly appointed provisional governor, Hamilton Gamble—Attorney General Edward Bates's brother-in-law—who warned in his inaugural address on August 1 that the state faced "not merely a war between different divisions of the State, but a war between neighbors" that threatened "that condition of anarchy, in which a man when he goes to bed with his family at night does not know whether he shall ever rise again, or whether his house shall remain intact until morning."[7]

Newly ensconced in St. Louis, Frémont wrote to Lincoln painting a grim picture of a state "in disorder, [with] nearly every county in an insurrectionary condition, and the enemy advancing in force, by different points of the southern frontier."[8] A bleak situation soon became more dire after a showdown in Springfield, Missouri, between a military force loyal to Governor Jackson and Union forces led by General Nathaniel Lyon, led to a disastrous defeat for the Union army and the death of General Lyon, the first Union general killed in the Civil War. The demoralized army's pell-mell retreat—leaving the dead general's body behind—spread fear that St. Louis could be next. Four days later, amid "whispers of rebel plots within the city," Frémont declared martial law in St. Louis.[9]

Against the backdrop of a rapidly deteriorating military situation and mounting criticism of his ineffectual leadership, Frémont decided, without consulting Lincoln or anybody else in the administration, to issue his August 30 proclamation. In addition to emancipating the slaves of disloyal owners, the edict declared martial law throughout Missouri, placed all "the administrative powers of the State" in Frémont's hands, and ordered that anyone captured with "arms in their hands" be tried by the military and, if found guilty, shot.[10]

Lincoln was blindsided by Frémont's emancipation order, which even Salmon Chase, the most antislavery member of Lincoln's cabinet, regarded as "an act of insubordination." It may be true, as Frémont's most famous biographer claims, that Frémont was more "impetuous" than "scheming," but Frémont knew full well that his emancipation edict was unlikely to meet with the president's approval, which is why he made no effort to consult beforehand with Lincoln or anyone else in the administration. When Frémont read the proclamation to his wife and a military aide (the only two people he consulted about the directive) on the morning of August 30th, the aide, a Quaker abolitionist and the son-in-law of Lucretia Mott, warned Frémont that "Mr. Seward will never allow this." Frémont seemed to act in the hope that while he would not be able to secure prior approval for such an order, Lincoln would have to accept it as a fait accompli because the costs of nullifying his proclamation once it had been broadcast to the nation would be too high for the new president.[11]

The idea of military emancipation was not a novelty. Liberating slaves in wartime as a way of weakening the enemy had a long pedigree dating back to antiquity. Most notably, the British used emancipation decrees in their efforts to subdue the rebellious colonists in the American Revolution. During the War of 1812, fears that the British would foment slave insurrections were widespread among southern slaveholders, an anxiety sharpened by memories of the recent slave revolt in Haiti. Fearing that military emancipations "might let loose unimaginable waves of violence," Americans had spent decades arguing that "the laws of war sharply separated the tobacco field from the battlefield," decrying military emancipations as "the very definition of savagery" and the antithesis of modern "civilized warfare."[12]

Admittedly Lincoln had countenanced some earlier moves against slavery by generals, most notably in the case of General Benjamin Butler, the newly appointed commander of Fortress Monroe, who in May 1861 refused to return three fugitive slaves to their Virginia owner, a colonel in the Confederate army. Since Virginia had seceded from the Union the day after the slaves escaped, Butler maintained that Virginians had forfeited their right to have slaves returned under the Fugitive Slave Law of 1850. As Butler explained to the officer who came to retrieve the slaves, "I am under no constitutional obligations to a foreign country, which Virginia now claims to be." And since slaves were being used to help build Confederate batteries that were firing on his troops, he believed it necessary as a military matter to withhold that labor from the Confederacy.[13]

Unlike Frémont, however, Butler immediately sought approval for his improvised policy. On May 25, less than forty-eight hours after the three slaves reached Fortress Monroe, Butler reported the events to higher-ups and sought approval for his decision. He issued no public proclamations and explicitly recognized that the ultimate fate of the runaways had to "be determined by policymakers in Washington," even proffering receipts for the runaway slaves so that the owner could reclaim them when the war was over. He also offered to return the slaves if the owner was ready to swear an oath of allegiance to the Union. As more slaves made their way to the safety of the Union fort, Butler again pressed the government for a statement clarifying the policy regarding rebel slaves who came within Union lines. Three days after his second entreaty—and a week after the first slaves reached Fortress Monroe—Lincoln convened his cabinet to consider "Butler's fugitive slave law." After the meeting, Secretary of War Simon Cameron telegraphed Butler with the administration's approval of his actions and a statement of policy. Union troops were not to interfere with slavery in the Confederate states, but slaves from those states who reached Union lines voluntarily, whether men, women, or children, did not necessarily need to be returned to their owners. This did not mean that those slaves would be emancipated, however. "The question of their final disposition," Cameron continued, "will be reserved for further determination."[14]

By the time Frémont issued his proclamation at the end of August, Congress had weighed in on the question, although in a limited way that did not explicitly address the "final disposition" of slaves who reached Union lines, reflecting the fact that most members of Congress doubted that the federal government had the constitutional power to interfere with slavery in the states. Indeed, at the same time the House and Senate passed the Confiscation Act, they overwhelmingly approved (with only five dissenting votes in the two bodies) a resolution that declared the purpose of the war was solely to uphold the supremacy of the Constitution and not "for the purpose of overthrowing or interfering with the rights or established institutions." Signed by Lincoln on August 6, 1861, the Confiscation Act authorized the military to confiscate only those slaves directly employed in Confederate war-making, which was a fraction of the many thousands of slaves coming into Union lines. Assiduously avoiding the language of emancipation, the law stipulated that a slaveowner "shall forfeit his claim" to a slave's labor if that slave were found to have been "required or permitted by the person to whom such labor or service is claimed to be due, or his lawful agent, to work or to be employed in or upon any fort, navy yard, dock, armory, ship, entrenchment, or in any military or naval service whatsoever, against the Government and lawful authority of the United States." The law, then, both explicitly limited the category of slaves who could be confiscated and declined to say explicitly that confiscated slaves would be freed.[15]

Lincoln signed the law "with great reluctance," although not because he disapproved of its limitations. Lincoln worried that despite its limited scope and careful language, the act would alienate the border states, whose congressional representatives were overwhelmingly and vocally opposed to the measure. Lincoln also believed the statute would be vulnerable to constitutional challenge for, among other things, permitting the taking of property without due process of law. He also worried that the act would be difficult if not impossible to enforce since neither the attorney general, federal district attorneys, or the army had the time or resources to determine definitively how slaves had been previously employed.[16]

Lincoln's misgivings about the Confiscation Act, however, paled in significance to his worries about Frémont's order, which was targeted at a border state still in the Union, applied to every slave of a disloyal owner, however those slaves were employed, and explicitly declared those slaves to be free. Lincoln was particularly concerned about the effect Frémont's order could have on Kentucky, a state with about 225,000 slaves. Only two months before, neighboring Tennessee, a state with only a slightly larger slave population than Kentucky, voted overwhelmingly to secede, becoming the eleventh (and, it turned out, final) state to do so.[17] Kentucky was also important because it was the ninth (Missouri was eighth, but with a slave population only half of Kentucky's) most populous state in the country; the only state that joined the Confederacy that had a larger population than Kentucky was Virginia.[18] In Lincoln's judgment, the North could not prevail in the Civil War if Kentucky seceded. "To lose Kentucky," he explained to an ally, "is nearly the same as to lose the whole game." With Kentucky gone, he feared that Missouri and perhaps even Maryland would follow, and then they might "as well consent to separation at once."[19]

From Lincoln's perspective, Frémont's timing could hardly have been worse. For months, Kentucky had pursued a policy of neutrality that the administration had generally respected by keeping Union troops out of the state. Lincoln's restraint seemed to pay dividends when a unionist slate triumphed in the state's congressional elections in June. By the end of the summer, it was clear that the state's neutrality policy was no longer tenable and the legislature seemed ready to side with the Union. At the same time, a large Confederate army had amassed on the Kentucky-Tennessee border poised to invade—an invasion that began on September 3—in hopes of bringing the state into the Confederacy. The last thing Lincoln needed was a "foolish" decree that could, his old friend Joshua Speed warned, "crush out every vestige of a union party in the state." At the stroke of a pen, Frémont seemed to risk undoing all of Lincoln's arduous work aimed at persuading Kentucky not to join the Confederacy.[20]

Despite his unhappiness with Frémont's rogue order, Lincoln's initial response was neither to fire the general nor to command that the order be rescinded. The president had the formal authority to do so, of course, but command came with substantial costs, as Lincoln well recognized. Instead, Lincoln opted for persuasion. In a "private and confidential" letter to Frémont, written "in a spirit of caution and not of censure," Lincoln related his "anxiety" about two aspects of the proclamation. The first of these was Frémont's order to execute all captured Confederates. Lincoln feared this would lead the enemy to retaliate in kind, and so he ordered Frémont not to shoot any captive without first receiving his approval. On the slavery question, though, Lincoln carefully avoided the language of command. Instead, he explained that the vow to liberate slaves "will alarm our Southern Union friends, and turn them against us" and "perhaps ruin our rather fair prospect for Kentucky." He therefore requested that Frémont, "as of your own motion," modify the order so as to conform to the Confiscation Act that Congress had passed the month before—that is, by limiting the order's scope to slaves directly employed in Confederate war-making.[21]

Lincoln's effort to persuade Frémont to modify the order failed. On September 10, a week after sending Frémont his letter, Lincoln received a truculent response, hand delivered by Frémont's wife Jessie, who arrived at the White House determined to persuade the president to sustain her husband's emancipation order.[22] In his reply, dated September 8, Frémont made no apologies for acting without first seeking the president's approval—or indeed "without consultation or advice with anyone." In war, a delay of even a day or two could make the difference between "success or disaster," Frémont lectured the president, and in issuing the proclamation he had followed his "best judgment" about what the precarious military situation in Missouri required. If Lincoln disagreed with that judgment, he would have to "openly direct [him] to make the correction" since "if I were to retract of my own accord it would imply that I myself thought it was wrong and that I had acted without the reflection which the gravity of the point demanded." That he was unwilling to do since he had "acted with full deliberation and upon the certain conviction that it was a measure right and necessary." The accolades showered upon Frémont after the edict only bolstered that conviction.[23]

So convinced was Frémont that his proclamation was right and necessary that even after receiving the president's request, he ordered the distribution of thousands of copies of the proclamation and issued deeds of manumission to about two dozen slaves.[24] Maybe the best measure of Frémont's chutzpah is that at the same time that he was defying Lincoln's request to modify the order, he was asking the president (in a separate letter, also dated September 10) to give him more power by extending his command to include Tennessee, Ohio, and Mississippi.[25]

Historians have understandably seen in Frémont's refusal to modify his order evidence of the general's "considerable stubbornness," a lifelong "rebellious streak," and a "quarrelsome" disposition. Even biographers sympathetic to Frémont admit the refusal was "foolish" and impolitic.[26] It didn't help Frémont's cause that in Jessie Frémont's audience with the president, she seemed to "hint . . . at her husband's superior wisdom and greater prestige," although Frémont's letter breathed a condescension and arrogance that hardly needed any amplification from his spouse.[27]

In the weeks prior to receiving Frémont's reply, Lincoln had already been made aware of deep flaws in Frémont's judgment and decision-making—and the upset it was causing in St. Louis. In the first few days of September, both Montgomery Blair and Frank Blair told the president that Frémont's case was "hopeless" and that he needed to be fired immediately—and for reasons unconnected to the proclamation.[28] The day before meeting with Jessie Frémont, Lincoln wrote to Major General David Hunter about the deficiencies in Frémont's leadership style. "His cardinal mistake," Lincoln wrote, "is that he isolates himself, and allows nobody to see him; and by which he does not know what is going on in the very matter he is dealing with." Lincoln asked (not commanded) Hunter, a division commander stationed in Chicago under Frémont's command, to take up a position "by [Frémont's] side" to help provide the uncooperative general the "assistance which it is difficult to give him."[29]

Now confronted with Frémont's defiant refusal on top of mounting evidence of his military and political shortcomings, Lincoln still would not countenance the firing of Frémont,[30] although he did write to Frémont ordering that the proclamation "be so modified, held, and construed, as to conform to, and not to transcend, the provisions on the same subject" in the first Confiscation Act. Even then, compliance was hardly immediate. On September 16, five days after Lincoln sent his letter, Frémont telegraphed the president informing him that he had not received the president's message but had seen it printed in the newspapers. "Shall I act on that?" he asked. No record exists of Lincoln's reply, if there was one, but army adjutant-general Lorenzo Thomas later informed Secretary of War Cameron that a week after receiving Lincoln's directive modifying the proclamation, Frémont ordered another "200 copies of the original proclamation . . . printed and sent immediately to Ironton," about ninety miles south of St. Louis, "for distribution through the country."[31]

The real problem for Lincoln, however, was less getting Frémont to comply with his order than getting backed into a corner in which he had to resort to a command that he knew would come at a high political cost. The barrage of criticism that followed Lincoln's modification of Frémont's order was unlike anything he had incurred in the first six months of his presidency. "The White House mailbag," notes Lincoln biographer Michael Burlingame, "overflowed with letters denouncing the revocation."[32]

Writing to Massachusetts senator Charles Sumner from his home in Cincinnati, the abolitionist writer and minister Moncure Conway could not disguise his disgust. "I cannot convey to you," he wrote, "the burning sense of wrong which is filling the breasts of our people here, as they gradually come to see that there is no President of the United States—only a President of Kentucky." In the *National Anti-Slavery Standard*, the official newspaper of the American Anti-Slavery Society, Boston's Edmund Quincy condemned Lincoln's order as "one of those blunders which are worse than crimes." William Lloyd Garrison, the abolitionist editor of the *Liberator*, the most widely circulated antislavery newspaper, charged the president with a "serious dereliction of duty" and condemned his order as "timid, depressing, suicidal." In private, Garrison was harsher still, fuming that while the president may have been six foot four, he was "only a dwarf in mind."[33]

But it was not only abolitionists who were fuming. A large swath of otherwise supportive Republicans were deeply unhappy with the president's order. Joseph Medill, the influential Republican editor of the *Chicago Tribune*, informed Treasury Secretary Chase that the president's "frightfully retrograde" directive had "cast a funeral gloom" not only over Chicago but over "the intire [*sic*] west." According to Medill, nothing that the previous president, James Buchanan, had done had ever "received so universal censure." John L. Scripps, author of a Lincoln campaign biography in 1860, informed the president that his order was received in the Northwest as "a backward step" that "has engendered doubts and impaired confidence, [and] has checked enlistments. . . . It is regarded as a retreat far more fatal than a retreat from a battlefield." Maine's Republican senator William Pitt Fessenden, who thought Lincoln's letter "very foolish," reported that among his constituents the president "has lost ground amazingly" as a result of the modification of Frémont's order.[34] Although there is no systematic public opinion polling from this time period, there seems little doubt that in September 1861 pollsters would have found a sharp drop in Lincoln's public approval across the North, particularly among core constituencies of the Republican Party.[35]

Even Lincoln's longtime friend and ally, Orville Browning, newly ensconced as a US senator and nobody's idea of a radical, complained bitterly about Lincoln's decision to modify Frémont's order. He echoed what Lincoln was hearing from nearly every quarter—namely, that Frémont's order "had the unqualified approval of every true friend of the Government" and that its revocation was "really filling the hearts of our friends with despondency." Browning posed the same question that so many others were asking the president: Why should "traitors who are warring upon the constitution and laws" receive protection of "their title to their slaves"? After all, if the government could take the life of a traitor, then surely it could seize the traitor's slaves. In Browning's view, there had "been too much tenderness toward traitors and rebels," and it was past time to "strike them terrible blows, and strike them hard and quick, or the government will go hopelessly to pieces."[36]

Lincoln expected to be roundly criticized in antislavery circles for revoking Frémont's emancipation order—which is why he initially tried to persuade Frémont to modify the order himself. However, Browning's letter came as a shock to Lincoln. Browning was a conservative when it came to most things, including slavery, as Lincoln well knew. A quarter century earlier, when the two men served together as Whigs in the Illinois state legislature, Browning, born and raised in Kentucky, authored resolutions that affirmed the "sacred" right to own slaves, resolutions that Lincoln refused to support.[37] Lincoln won the Republican presidential nomination in 1860 by staking out a moderate stance on slavery that made him an acceptable second choice for different wings of the party. Browning's response suggested that Lincoln now found himself in a position outside the mainstream of his party.

Stung by his friend's criticism, Lincoln penned a lengthy reply justifying the modification of Frémont's order and pleading for Browning's support "on the grounds which you and other kind friends gave me the election." Lincoln reminded Browning that in modifying the order he was adhering to the Confiscation Act passed by Congress just weeks before, an act that Browning and virtually every Republican had voted for. Lincoln acknowledged that under military law a general could seize property, including slaves, for military purposes, but that did not give him the authority to "fix their permanent future condition." That was the job of policymakers in Congress, not rogue generals. The question of whether slaves should be liberated, Lincoln insisted, was "purely political, and not within the range of military law, or necessity." To allow Frémont or even the president to emancipate slaves—as opposed to confiscating them for the duration of the war—would be to succumb to "dictatorship." Whereas Browning saw Frémont's order as "the only means of saving the government," Lincoln believed that allowing Frémont or even the president to "make permanent rules of property by proclamation" would be "itself the surrender of the government."[38]

For most of the first six months of the war, as legal historian John Fabian Witt notes, Lincoln had "tried his best to avoid the question of whether he could free the South's slaves." It's not that Lincoln doubted that slavery was morally wrong. The Republican Party he helped form was dedicated to halting slavery's spread and bringing about its eventual extinction. And he understood as well as anyone that slavery, that "vast and far reaching disturbing element," was the root cause of the

Civil War. But he also believed that as president, the less he said about slavery the better the chances of bringing a quick end to the war and restoring the Union. As he explained to one of the many who applauded Frémont's action, "We didn't go into the war to put down slavery, but to put the flag back, and to act differently at this moment would ... not only weaken our cause but smack of bad faith." As his letter to Browning makes clear, Lincoln recoiled from the idea that the war gave him or any of his generals the authority to abolish slavery with the stroke of a pen.[39]

Lincoln's understanding of presidential power frustrated the likes of Sumner, who could see no point in having "the power of a God if not to use it God-like." But for Lincoln there was nothing godlike about presidential power. Even if he were so inclined to issue an edict from upon high declaring slaves free, it would not abolish slavery. Nothing would stop the federal courts, which were stacked with Democrats hostile to Lincoln and sympathetic to the rights of slaveowners, from siding with aggrieved slaveowners and annulling such an order, especially once the military emergency had passed. And a godlike edict would count for little if it lost Lincoln the political support of the border states, enabling the Confederacy to secure its independence and preserve slavery. The power of the presidency, Lincoln understood, even in wartime, was the power to persuade.[40]

Frémont's order and the firestorm of criticism that followed Lincoln's modification of that order demonstrated that his initial strategy of studied ambiguity and avoidance was no longer viable. During the fall of 1861, as the prospect of a speedy end to the war receded, Lincoln was compelled to think more deeply about what to do about slavery. Proceeding with "all due caution," Lincoln began to formulate his own plan to end slavery, one that he hoped would unite the country and strengthen the Union; uphold democracy, the Constitution, and the rule of law; and harness the president's power of persuasion rather than rely on unilateral commands.[41]

CHAPTER 2

A Failure to Persuade

Lincoln's Plan for Compensated Emancipation in the Border States

Early in November 1861, Lincoln summoned to the White House Delaware's sole congressional representative, George P. Fisher. With fewer than eighteen hundred slaves in a state of well over one hundred thousand people, Delaware had far less to lose from the abolition of slavery than any other state, and the cost to the federal government of compensating slaveowners would be relatively small. Delaware had also at times flirted with emancipation. A decade and a half earlier, the state legislature came within one vote of passing a law that would have provided for the gradual emancipation of the state's slaves.[1]

Lincoln wanted Fisher, a one-time Whig who was broadly antislavery, to help him introduce a plan of gradual, compensated emancipation in the state legislature. Fisher agreed, and Lincoln drafted two alternative bills. One version phased out slavery over a five-year period, while the other allowed three decades for the phase-out. Lincoln preferred the latter plan, although he told Fisher that he was happy to go with a ten-year plan instead. What mattered to Lincoln was not the precise number of years but getting a state to commit to compensated emancipation.[2]

Lincoln also secured Fisher's assistance in setting up a White House meeting with a prominent Delaware slaveholder, Benjamin Burton. Lincoln believed that if he could persuade the state's largest slaveholder—a Republican—to back his plan for gradual, compensated emancipation, then others in the state would follow his lead. If Delaware were to initiate such a plan, he assured Burton, "all the other border states will accept it." And with the border states committed to gradual emancipation, the Confederacy would be forced to give up the fight.³ In Lincoln's view, his plan was "the cheapest and most humane way of ending the war and saving lives." When Burton expressed skepticism that Congress would fund the plan, Lincoln brushed aside the concern, telling Burton, "You tend to your end of the swingle tree and I'll tend to mine."⁴

Lincoln exuded confidence that he could win over Congress to his plan of compensated emancipation if the border states committed to a plan of gradual emancipation. At the end of November, he assured Massachusetts senator Charles Sumner, who was urging the president to embrace emancipation, that "in a month or six weeks we should all be together" on the matter of slavery.⁵ On the afternoon of December 1, the day before the 37th Congress was to meet for its first regular session since the beginning of the war, Lincoln told his friend and confidant, Illinois senator Orville Browning, that he was "very hopeful of ultimate success."⁶ He suggested that "the policy of paying Delaware, Maryland, Kentucky & Missouri $500 a piece [for their slaves] ... should work the extinction of slavery in twenty years," and at a fraction of the financial cost that "was necessary to support the war for one year." Lincoln also agreed with Browning that the plan of gradual, compensated emancipation should include "a scheme of colonizing the blacks somewhere on the American Continent."⁷

In his first annual message, delivered on December 3, 1861, Lincoln made no mention of his Delaware scheme but he floated the idea of Congress adopting "some mode of valuation" in the "not impossible" event that some slave states were willing to embrace emancipation. He also recommended that "steps be taken" for colonizing all freed slaves "at some place, or places, in a climate congenial to them" and encouraged Congress to appropriate money to acquire new territory where emancipated slaves could be sent. He even suggested that the nation's "free colored people" might be included in the colonization scheme, at least on a voluntary basis.⁸

Lincoln's hope of crafting a broadly acceptable compromise that "made slaveholders partners in, rather than opponents of, emancipation" ran into immediate difficulties in Delaware. Fisher and his state legislative allies, who proposed a ten-year phase-out plan, found that Lincoln's arguments—and the promise of roughly $500 a slave in compensation to slaveholders as well as a pledge to help colonize the emancipated—made limited headway against the state's engrained racism. Even those who "look[ed] upon slavery as a curse ... look[ed] upon freedom possessed by a negro ... as a greater curse."[9] By February, it was clear that the bill could not pass and the plan was abandoned.[10]

Undeterred by the setback in Delaware, Lincoln sent a message to Congress on March 6, 1862, in which he recommended adoption of a joint resolution that pledged to compensate any state that adopted the "gradual abolishment of slavery."[11] Having Congress publicly commit to compensation, Lincoln hoped, would help to overcome border states' misgivings about gradual emancipation. Although "merely initiatory," Lincoln's plan offered something for everyone. It envisioned "gradual, and not sudden emancipation," which was "better for all." It did not infringe on the states' constitutional right to set their own policies regarding slavery. It was far more cost effective than fighting a war, as "any member of Congress, with the census-tables and Treasury-reports before him, can readily see for himself." Moreover, if the border states committed to gradual emancipation, it would deprive the Confederacy of hope that the border states would join them, which "substantially ends the rebellion." And, finally, Lincoln warned, there was no foreseeing "all the incidents [and] all the ruin" that might result from the war's prolonged continuation.[12]

Lincoln's message was widely praised across the North.[13] The fervently antislavery Illinois representative Owen Lovejoy hailed it for having "presented ground where all [Republicans] might stand, the conservative and radical." However, border state representatives in Congress appeared unmoved by Lincoln's words. On March 9, a disappointed Lincoln summoned Missouri congressman Frank Blair to his office to complain that not one member of Congress from a border state had uttered even "one word to [him] about it." Lincoln told Blair that he wanted "a frank and direct talk" with the border state members so that he could impress upon them the many virtues of his plan. If they would only embrace it, Lincoln told Blair, "the war will cease" and there would be "no further need for standing armies among them." It would also relieve Lincoln of the increasingly vexing problem of what to do with the fleeing slaves who crossed into Union army lines. Blair was skeptical the president would make much headway but agreed to arrange a meeting at the White House the next morning with as many border state representatives as he could round up.[14]

At the meeting with the border state delegation, Lincoln elaborated on the arguments he had made in his congressional message and assured the members that while he would "lament their refusal" to accept his plan, he had "no designs beyond the action of the States on this particular subject." However, all of Lincoln's reasons and reassurances did little to soften border state resistance. Maryland's John Crisfield told Lincoln that while his constituents might be open to emancipation, they would only back the plan if they were guaranteed that "they could be rid of the race." Missouri's John Noell was sympathetic, but even he felt it might be unnecessary because "natural causes . . . would, at no distant day, extinguish [slavery]." A few like Kentucky's Charles Wickliffe raised constitutional objections to the idea of Congress appropriating funds to buy slaves, and those who did not find constitutional obstacles worried that, as a political matter, the border states did not "like to be coerced into Emancipation," even if it was "by indirection." The meeting was civil and respectful, but the president failed to win many converts, as became clear two days later when the border state representatives caucused and the great majority "angrily rejected emancipation, 'whether coated with sugar or gunpowder.'"[15]

Although Congress ultimately approved Lincoln's joint resolution,[16] border state representatives opposed the resolution with "almost perfect unanimity," and without border state buy-in the resolution's offer of compensation was essentially meaningless. Indeed, pressing for gradual compensated emancipation seemed only to harden opposition. In Kentucky, the state legislature attempted to have "disenfranchised for life" anyone who "may advocate the doctrine of the abolition or emancipation of slavery."[17] In Maryland, where "legislators never really considered the proposal," even some of Lincoln's own appointees came to regard anyone who supported the president's plan to be "an abolitionist and not worthy of the confidence of any gentleman."[18] At a state constitutional convention in Missouri in June 1862, those sympathetic to Lincoln proposed a compensated emancipation amendment that would have phased out slavery over a twenty-five-year period; the amendment was resoundingly defeated, receiving less than a quarter of the vote. Northern Democrats, meanwhile, continued to pillory Lincoln's plan for "purchasing the slaves of other people, and turning them loose in their midst."[19]

Despite the stiffening border state opposition, Lincoln was still not ready to give up on his plan, even while he was becoming increasingly frustrated by border state legislators' unwillingness to act on it. In his May proclamation revoking General David Hunter's audacious emancipation decree, which declared every slave in South Carolina, Georgia, and Florida "forever free," Lincoln took the opportunity to appeal directly and "earnestly ... to the people in the [border] states." He pleaded with them to adopt "a calm and enlarged consideration" of the matter and to rise "above personal and partizan politics." Implicitly contrasting the moderation and reasonableness of his plan with the sanctimoniousness of some abolitionists, Lincoln said his plan "acts not the pharisee"—instead, it "makes common cause for a common object, casting no reproaches upon any." The change that his plan would bring about "would come gently as the dews of heaven, not rending or wrecking anything," unlike war's "remorseless revolutionary struggle" that he had warned against in his first annual message. Now was their opportunity to do more good than had "been done, by one effort, in all past time." "May the vast future not have to lament that you have neglected it," he admonished the people of the border states.[20]

Lincoln's appeal, however, fell on deaf ears. As spring turned to summer, his hope for a broadly acceptable accord with border states that would shorten the war and put the nation on a gradual but irreversible course of emancipation seemed increasingly untenable. The unprecedented carnage at the Battle of Shiloh in April 1862 extinguished hopes for a quick end to the war.[21] More dispiriting was the abject failure of General George McClellan's Peninsular Campaign, which never came close to achieving its objective of capturing the Confederate capital of Richmond. Unhappy with the Army of the Potomac's lack of progress, Lincoln visited McClellan in early July at his encampment on the James River in Virginia and came away "grieved," doubting the general's political loyalties and judgment and certain that he "would not fight."[22]

With the congressional session nearing its close, Lincoln "resolved to make one more earnest effort with the delegations from the border States to initiate a policy of voluntary emancipation by those States." On the steam sloop back to the nation's capital on July 10, Lincoln prepared a "carefully written speech" that he wanted to deliver to the border state representatives, who he believed possessed "more power for good than any other equal number of members."[23] Twenty-eight border state representatives and senators—six of whom were loyalists from Virginia and Tennessee—came to the White House on Saturday, July 12, to hear the president make his final pitch.[24]

In his "Appeal," Lincoln said he intended "no reproach or complaint," yet he told them bluntly that it was his view that "if you all had voted for the resolution in the gradual emancipation message of last March, the war would now be substantially ended." Lincoln understood that they held out hope that slavery would emerge from the war "without disturbance," but he told them that hope was no longer realistic. In classic Neustadtian fashion, the president tried to get the border state congressmen to see that what he wanted of them was "what their own appraisal of their own responsibilities requires them to do in their interest, not his."

> If the war continues long, as it must, . . . [slavery] will be extinguished by mere friction and abrasion—by the mere incidents of war. It will be gone, and you will have nothing valuable in lieu of it. . . . How much better for you and your people, to take the step which, at once, shortens the war, and secures substantial compensation for that which is sure to be wholly lost. . . . How much better for you, as seller, and the nation as buyer, to sell out, and buy out, that without which the war could never have been, than to sink both the thing to be sold, and the price of it, in cutting one another's throats.

The war would inevitably bring immediate emancipation without compensation, and so the only rational course, which would benefit both the border states and the nation, was for the border states to take the money that was being offered them and ensure a more gradual, orderly process of emancipation.[25]

Lincoln made it clear that the time for delay and deliberation had come to an end. He needed "a *decision* at once," although he stressed that he was not asking for immediate emancipation, only a commitment "to emancipate *gradually*." He also underscored his support for making colonization, so long as it was voluntary, an integral part of the plan. "Room in South America for colonization," he argued, "can be obtained cheaply, and in abundance." As for the lack of enthusiasm for colonization among Blacks, Lincoln suggested that "when numbers shall be large enough to be company and encouragement for one another, the freed people will not be so reluctant to go." The larger the scale, the more successful the enterprise would be.[26]

Reflecting the much greater urgency that he now felt, Lincoln wielded the threat of more radical action that he had played down in the meeting in March. He reminded the border state representatives that in repudiating General Hunter's emancipation directive, he had given "dissatisfaction, if not offence, to many whose support the country can not afford to lose." Moreover, he warned that the enormous "pressure" on him to use his powers as commander in chief to free the slaves "is still upon me, and is increasing." He made clear that he overturned Hunter's directive not because he disagreed with his general about slavery. Far from it. He and Hunter shared a "wish that all men everywhere could be free." Instead he nullified the military order of an "honest man" because he adjudged that allowing the order to stand would do more harm than good to the war effort. Lincoln left the border states in no doubt that as the pressures on him mounted he might arrive at a different calculus about what the successful prosecution of the war required.[27]

Lincoln knew that getting the border states representatives to approve his plan was a long shot but he beseeched them "at the least, [to] commend it to the consideration of your states and people." Lincoln had persevered in pushing his border state plan even when its chance of approval seemed slim because he genuinely believed that it was still by far the best path forward for the nation, both in the short term and the longer run. The day after the meeting, Lincoln blurted out to two of his stalwart antislavery allies in the House, Isaac Arnold and Owen Lovejoy: "Oh, if the border States would accept my proposition! Then ... you, Lovejoy and Arnold, and all of us, would not have lived in vain!

The labor of your life, Lovejoy, would be crowned with success—you would live to see the end of slavery."[28]

The great majority of border state representatives, however, remained unpersuaded. Following a "stormy" caucus, twenty of the border state representatives, including a few who had voted for Lincoln's plan in March, signed onto a lengthy reply that defended the members' previous vote against Lincoln's plan and refuted the arguments Lincoln had presented in his new Appeal. The representatives had done the math that Lincoln had asked them to do in March, and they calculated the cost of compensation and colonization to be prohibitive, especially at a time when the treasury was already "reeling under the enormous expenditure of the war." The price tag of Lincoln's plan was so high that the resolution was "but the annunciation of a sentiment which could not, or was not likely to be [made into] an actual tangible proposition." If the president really wanted the people of the border states to seriously consider a change as radical as emancipation, Congress needed first to "provide sufficient funds and place them at your disposal" so that the affected states would be guaranteed to "reap the fruits of the promise."[29]

Their objections, though, went deeper. The representatives questioned why those who had loyally supported the government should be the ones to yield their inviolable and undisputed "right to hold slaves." They rubbished Lincoln's claim that had they voted for the resolution the war would be "substantially ended"; after all, the resolution passed even without their support. And there was no reason to think the fighting ardor of the Confederacy would have been diminished by emancipation in the border states; if anything, they said, it would only redouble the enemy's resolve to fight to protect the institution of slavery. Lincoln's plan, moreover, was unnecessary for the border states to demonstrate their loyalty to the Union since they were already "fixed unalterably" in their adherence to the Union. What was needed to defeat the secessionists was not for the border states to adopt Lincoln's plan of gradual emancipation but for Lincoln to "confine [himself] to [his] constitutional authority: confine [his] subordinates within the same limits; [and] conduct this war solely for the purpose of restoring the constitution to its legitimate authority."[30]

The border state reply made clear what Lincoln should have known by now: that whatever its merits in his own mind, his plan was not politically viable. Indeed, his secretary of the navy Gideon Welles recalled this "last fruitless and hopeless interview" with the border state congressmen as the pivotal point at which Lincoln became convinced that his policy needed to change and that the "emancipation of the slaves in the rebel States must precede that in the border States."[31] Welles's recollection is not entirely accurate as Lincoln was still not ready to give up on the idea of compensated emancipation in the border states.[32] In fact, on July 14, in direct response to the border states' reply, Lincoln submitted to Congress draft legislation—rather than a mere resolution—that appropriated funds and made it the duty of the president to use those funds to compensate slaveowners in states that committed to immediate or gradual emancipation.[33] Although a bill modeled on Lincoln's draft bill was reported out of committee, Congress adjourned on July 17 without voting on a bill that many Republicans, "sick of this dickering, bargaining business," found "ridiculous."[34] Lincoln's plan seemed dead, his efforts at persuasion an almost total failure.

CHAPTER 3

A Painful Last Resort

Lincoln's Decision to Emancipate

In the days following his July 12th meeting with the border state representatives, Lincoln was forced not only to reckon with the collapse of his plan for compensated emancipation but with how to respond to the Second Confiscation Act, which, after seven months of intense debate and many amendments, finally emerged from a congressional conference committee.[1] The act contained multitudes, including authorizing the president to employ "persons of African descent" in the war effort in any way he deemed "necessary and proper" (Section 11), while also authorizing the president to transport to "some tropical country" those very same "persons of the African race," so long as they were willing to go (Section 12). At the heart of the measure, though, was Section 9, which declared that any slave in the Confederacy who came within the Union army's control—either by fleeing from Confederate-held territory or as a result of the Union army gaining control of territory—would instantly become "forever free of their servitude, and not again held as slaves." This went well beyond the First Confiscation Act, which was limited in scope to slaves who were directly employed in the Confederate war effort and which did not explicitly stipulate that freedom would extend beyond the duration of the war. In passing the Second Confiscation Act, as historian James Oakes emphasizes, "Republicans in Congress . . . made it clear that . . . they intended to destroy slavery completely in the seceded states."[2]

Border state representatives were "scandalized by the vast implications" of the act, but even some Republicans worried it went too far.

Orville Browning presented the final bill to the president on July 14th and urged a veto. At stake, he told Lincoln, was "whether he was to control the abolitionists and radicals, or whether they were to control him." Signing the bill, Browning insisted, would be a political disaster for the administration, especially in the border states. In contrast, a veto would "raise a storm of enthusiasm in support of the Administration in the border states which would be worth to us 100,000 muskets."[3] Secretary of State William Henry Seward and Secretary of War Edwin Stanton also counseled a veto. Stanton argued that the bill was plainly unconstitutional because, as Lincoln had long recognized, the Constitution did not give Congress the power to legislate about slavery in the states. Stanton also took aim at provisions in the law that enabled the government to permanently seize all property belonging to any person found to have "engaged in rebellion, or who has given aid or comfort thereto." According to Stanton, since the law took property not only from the traitor but the traitor's heirs, it violated Article III, section 3, of the Constitution, which stipulated that "no Attainder of Treason shall work Corruption of Blood, or Forfeiture, except during the Life of the Person attainted."[4]

Lincoln had never liked the First Confiscation Act and did little to enforce it, and he was no more happy about the Second Confiscation Act, which, like the first, seemed, in the words of Ohio Senator John Sherman, "more useful as a declaration of policy than as an act to be enforced."[5] But the act also reflected a growing desire for "sterner measures," and congressional Republicans had voted overwhelmingly for the compromise measure, whatever its faults and ambiguities. Lincoln knew that a veto could fracture the party he led.[6]

Lincoln was uncertain what to do. On the morning of July 15, he asked Congress to delay its pending adjournment so that it would have a chance to remedy the bill in case he chose to veto it. He then shut himself in his library to compose a veto message. Visiting Lincoln that morning, Browning found the president "looked weary, care-worn, and troubled." When Browning expressed sympathy for the "the troubles [that] crowded so heavily upon him," a "very sad" Lincoln said, "in a very tender and touching tone, 'Browning I must die sometime.'"[7]

News of a possible veto enraged the bill's most ardent supporters who "stormed into the White House" and warned Lincoln's private secretary John Nicolay that with a veto the president "destroys the Republican party and ruins his administration." After a series of private meetings with members of Congress, Lincoln reached an accord: he would sign the bill if Congress passed a resolution making clear that any land seized by the government could not be retained after the owner's death and must instead revert to the owner's heirs. Having secured the resolution, Lincoln signed the bill into law on July 17, although he took the highly unusual step of transmitting his veto message as well, a step that so angered some Republicans that they "retaliated against Lincoln by filibustering a motion to print his veto message."[8]

Whatever Lincoln's misgivings about the efficacy and wisdom of the Second Confiscation Act, the collapse of his border state plan together with General George McClellan's embarrassing setbacks in the Peninsular Campaign had clearly prompted a shift in his thinking about how best to deal with slavery. According to Welles, it was on Sunday, July 13, the day after his fruitless meeting with the border state representatives, that Lincoln first raised the possibility of using his formal powers of command to emancipate slaves by proclamation. After having given the matter "much thought," the president said, he had "about come to the conclusion" that emancipation of slaves in the Confederacy was "a military necessity absolutely essential for the salvation of the Union." This was, Welles noted, "a new departure" for the president, who "until this time, . . . whenever the question of emancipation . . . had been in any way alluded to, . . . had been prompt and emphatic in denouncing any interference by the general government" with slavery in the states. Unable to persuade the border states to commit to gradual emancipation, Lincoln was being pushed by events and shifting sentiments within his party to rely on his powers of command to win the war and bring about the demise of slavery.[9]

At a cabinet meeting on Tuesday, July 22, 1862, with Congress now out of town, Lincoln unveiled his new departure. He announced that he planned to issue a proclamation that would emancipate "all slaves in the States which should then be in rebellion." He explained that after he read them his draft proclamation, he wished for a "free discussion." Not up for discussion, however, was whether or not to issue the edict.

On that question, he was "settled in his own mind." The "order" was "his own scheme," he told them, and the "responsibility of the measure was his."¹⁰

The draft proclamation consisted of three parts. The first part complied with the Second Confiscation Act's requirement (Section 6) that the president issue a proclamation warning that after sixty days the federal government could seize "all the estate and property, moneys, stocks, and credits" of anyone still "participating in, aiding, countenancing, or abetting" the rebellion. The second part—showing that he still had not given up on his border state policy—announced Lincoln's intention, when Congress convened in December, to again recommend his plan for compensating states that voluntarily adopted the gradual abolishment of slavery. The final part, one sentence of eighty-five words, dropped the bombshell, ordering, "as Commander-in-Chief of the Army and Navy of the United States," that on January 1, 1863, "all persons held as slaves" in areas under Confederate control shall "then, thenceforward, and forever be free."¹¹ Lincoln would do by command what he had failed to do by persuasion.

When Lincoln finished, there was an awkward silence. Attorney General Edward Bates was the first to speak. A Missouri politician and longtime supporter of colonization, Bates said he supported the plan so long as it could be joined to compulsory "deportation" of freed slaves. Treasury Secretary Salmon Chase, the most strongly antislavery member in the cabinet, was lukewarm at best, warning the president that the emancipation decree would be legally vulnerable and would result in "depredation and massacre" across the South. Postmaster General Montgomery Blair slammed the decree as a political disaster that would doom the party in the upcoming midterm elections. The only other cabinet member to offer a view was Seward, who deemed the proclamation an unnecessary political and legal risk since the war itself would destroy slavery. Moreover, issuing it now would make the government look weak, as if this was "the last measure of an exhausted government, a cry for help" to the slaves. Perhaps, Seward suggested, it would be better if the proclamation was issued after a Union victory.¹²

Lincoln listened attentively to his cabinet's responses but after the meeting assured his secretary of war, who favored the proclamation's immediate release, that "it was his intention on the following day to issue his proclamation." He was done with persuasion and half-steps; it was time for decisive, unilateral presidential action. But even as he readied his command, the weakness of his position forced him to bargain.[13]

That evening, Seward, seeking reinforcements to bolster his case for delay, brought the old master Whig politico Thurlow Weed to see the president. Weed zeroed in on Lincoln's gravest concern, warning the president that his proclamation would likely do more harm than good and could very well "occasion serious disaffection to the Union in border States." Echoing Seward, he told Lincoln it was "more prudent to wait on events." The following morning Lincoln found on his desk a "blistering letter" from his postmaster general, a Marylander, that warned "even more luridly" of the cataclysmic political ramifications of the proclamation.[14]

"Paralyzed" by the appeals of his subordinates and allies, and beset by his own doubts about the "difficulty [of] foreseeing the [proclamation's] effects upon the people of the border States," Lincoln changed course, agreeing, at least for now, to set aside the proclamation. Instead he would release only the first paragraph as required by the Second Confiscation Act, which he did on Friday, July 25. Before he could issue the Emancipation Proclamation, he would first need to persuade his cabinet and the American people that his order was indeed, as he claimed in the draft proclamation, "a fit and necessary military measure."[15]

CHAPTER 4

A Failure to Persuade (Again)
Lincoln's Colonization Plan

By far the most famous of the persuasive efforts aimed at preparing the public for the Emancipation Proclamation was Lincoln's frequently quoted reply to Horace Greeley on August 22, 1862, in which he proclaimed, "If I could save the Union without freeing *any* slave I would do it, and if I could save it by freeing *all* the slaves I would do that; and if I could save it by freeing some and leaving others alone I would also do that."[1] Less often remembered is that Greeley's open letter to the president (printed in the *New York Tribune* under the headline "The Prayer of Twenty Millions") was, in part, a response to an initiative Lincoln undertook earlier in the month to allay White fears about emancipation by focusing on the idea of colonization raised by Edward Bates in the July 22nd cabinet meeting. Like Bates, Lincoln had long supported colonization, although unlike Bates he did not favor compulsory colonization. Just as he had tried to persuade border state slaveowners to accept the idea of compensated gradual emancipation, Lincoln now set out, for the first time, to persuade Blacks to voluntarily leave the country. But whereas the prior efforts at persuasion had been aimed at averting a unilateral executive proclamation of emancipation, the latter exercise in persuasion was principally aimed at making a proclamation of emancipation more palatable to Whites.

Colonization had always been an implicit and sometimes explicit part of the president's border state plan. Although Lincoln resisted Bates's urging to include colonization in the plan he recommended to Congress in March, he had included colonization in his annual message the previous December, and it remained an integral part of the discussion of the president's border state plan. Kentucky senator Garrett Davis, one of the few border state politicians to vote for the March joint resolution, explained that he did so because he had received "satisfactory assurance" that the government would not only compensate slaveowners for their loss but finance the colonization of freed Blacks. In the debate over emancipation in the District of Columbia in April, some pro-emancipation, anti-colonization Republicans backed a voluntary colonization provision in the bill only because they feared the president, who was concerned about the effect the legislation would have on Maryland and the other border states, "would veto the measure without it."[2]

If colonization was important to securing support for gradual abolition in a handful of border states, it loomed even larger in the effort to prepare Whites in the North to accept the emancipation of slaves in the Confederacy, a connection underscored in a letter Lincoln received from assistant interior secretary John P. Usher on August 2, 1862, endorsing the Chiriquí region (in what is now Panama) as a destination for Black emigration. If adopted, Usher said, the Chiriquí plan will "relieve the free states of the apprehension now prevailing, and fostered by the disloyal, that they are to be overrun by negroes made free by the war."[3]

After receiving Usher's letter, Lincoln named James Mitchell, a Methodist minister from Indiana, as Commissioner of Emigration, and tasked him with orchestrating a White House meeting with a representative group of Black leaders on the subject of colonization.[4] On Sunday, August 10, Mitchell spread the word to the city's Black churches that the president wished to confer with Black leaders about the more than half a million dollars that Congress had appropriated for colonization. A request by the president to meet with a delegation of African Americans was, if not unprecedented, highly unusual, and so on August 14 representatives from the city's Black churches and "several other interested persons" met with Mitchell at the Union Bethel AME Church to consider the offer to meet with Lincoln.[5]

Mitchell encountered considerable skepticism about the wisdom of the proposed meeting, but ultimately, with the help of *National Republican* editor Jacob Van Vleet, prevailed upon the group to send a five-person delegation to meet with Lincoln as "a gesture of respect for the president." At the same time, the group passed two resolutions expressing the depth of their reservations: the first declared that emigration was, at least at this moment in time, "inexpedient, inauspicious, and impolitic"; the second stated that it would be "unauthorized and unjust" for this small group to "compromise the interests of over four-and-a-half millions of our race by precipitate action on our part." Having recorded their reservations about the meeting, the group dispatched the five delegates, all "members of Washington's well-organized and well-educated antebellum black elite," to accompany Mitchell to the White House.[6]

As the delegation filed into the president's office, Lincoln greeted them "with great kindness, shaking hands very cordially with each one." For the next hour, the five men listened while Lincoln talked. The first important question to be answered, he forthrightly told them, was: "Why should they leave this country?" Lincoln explained, "You and we are different races. We have between us a broader difference than exists between almost any other two races." The result, "whether it is right or wrong," was "a great disadvantage to us both, as . . . your race suffer very greatly, many of them by living among us, while ours suffer from your presence." That "we suffer on each side," Lincoln argued, "affords a reason at least why we should be separated." Lincoln underscored his belief that enslaved Blacks were "suffering . . . the greatest wrong inflicted on any people," but once slavery was abolished, he cautioned, "you are yet far removed from being placed on an equality with the white race." Nowhere on "this broad continent," Lincoln observed, is "your race . . . made equal of a single man of ours. Go where you are treated the best, and the ban is still upon you." White racism ran so deep that Blacks would never be treated equally. Slavery was a terrible injustice, but it could and would be abolished. Systemic racism, on the other hand, was an injustice that Blacks would never be free of so long as they lived in the United States.[7]

Lincoln noted that one of "the principal difficulties in the way of colonization" was that the free Black person who could most readily leave "cannot see that his comfort would be advanced by" emigrating, whereas the Black slave who would readily exchange his chains for freedom elsewhere was not able to take advantage of the $600,000 Congress had appropriated for colonization. Free Blacks, he said, and he meant this in "no unkind sense," were taking "an extremely selfish view of the case." By agreeing to leave the country, they would "give a start to white people" who, "harsh as it may be," are unwilling "for you free colored people to remain with us." By showing that colonization was a viable solution, the free Black population could help Whites accept the end of slavery. They would also make the colonization project more successful since it would be so much better to start with "intelligent colored men, such as are before me," rather than those "whose intellects are clouded by Slavery." Lincoln implored them "to do something to help those who are not so fortunate as yourselves." "For the sake of your race," Lincoln insisted, "you should sacrifice something of your present comfort . . . to ameliorate the condition of those who have been subject to the hard usage of the world."[8]

Lincoln then pitched the advantages of establishing a colony in Central America, which was much closer than far-off Liberia and so would be more attractive to those who "would rather remain within reach of the country of your nativity." Sounding like a sales representative, Lincoln extolled the virtues of Chiriquí as a destination. It was, he assured them, "on a great line of travel," with "among the finest [harbors] in the world" and possessed of "very rich coal mines," which would provide colonists with "immediate employment" and "the means . . . for your self-reliance." There was no guarantee of success, of course, but, Lincoln exhorted, "we cannot succeed unless we try."[9]

Lincoln closed the monologue with a "practical" ask. Could they help him to "get a hundred tolerably intelligent men, with their wives and children" who would be willing to embark on such a venture? Or even fifty? Bargaining himself down, he offered that even "if I could find twenty-five able-bodied men, with a mixture of women and children . . . I think I could make a successful commencement." Even the smallest step forward could help him show that colonization was a viable solution to the problem of race in a post-emancipation America. At the end of the president's speech, the delegation's chair, Edward Thomas, told the president that "they would hold a consultation and in short time give an answer." Perhaps worried that his proposal might meet a quick rejection, Lincoln replied, "Take your full time—no hurry at all."[10]

If Lincoln hoped that his arguments would help to persuade Black opinion leaders to back colonization, he was to be disappointed. Granted he got encouraging news back from Thomas, who informed the president on August 16th that while the delegation had initially been "entirely hostile" to colonization, the president had brought them around by having so "ably brought [out] all the advantages" of the plan. Thomas proposed to confer next with "leading colored men" in Philadelphia, New York, and Boston,[11] but it turned out he did not speak for all of the five-person delegation and certainly not for the group that had reluctantly selected the delegates in the first place. Criticism of Thomas and the delegation was "rampant" among the Black community in the nation's capital.[12]

When Lincoln's comments were published in the newspapers the following day—as Lincoln clearly intended they would be since he had taken the unusual step of inviting a stenographer into the room—the reaction among many Black opinion leaders—as well as the broader antislavery community—was sharply negative. One wrote from Philadelphia to condemn the president for talking about "two races" when "in the matter of rights, there is but one race, and that is the human race." Among the most unsparing judgments came from Frederick Douglass, who slammed the president for sounding every bit the "ridiculous" and condescending "itinerant colonization lecturer" with their characteristic "contempt for negroes and . . . canting hypocrisy." Douglass and others found particularly offensive Lincoln's comment that seemed to lay the blame for the war on Black people's presence in the United States ("But for your race among us there could not be war," Lincoln had told the delegation). "It is not the presence of the Negro that causes this foul and unnatural war," Douglas retorted, "but the cruel and brutal cupidity of those who wish to possess . . . Negroes." Others expressed alarm that Lincoln's words would "arouse prejudice" and "increase enmity against" Blacks, a concern that seemed vindicated by reports from northern Blacks that after Lincoln's remarks were published they were "repeatedly insulted, and told that we must leave the country." A dismayed Salmon Chase recorded in his diary, "How much better would be a manly protest against prejudice against color."[13]

Ultimately, as historian Eric Foner observes, Lincoln's attempt to persuade Blacks to leave their country of their birth met with "the same result as Lincoln's conference a month earlier with the border congressmen: failure." As with the border states, the more Lincoln pressed his case for voluntary emigration, the more opposition seemed to harden. The core problem with Lincoln's emigration scheme was that no amount of talk could make viable a scheme that was, at its core, hopelessly impractical. There were in fact many Black Americans, including two of Frederick Douglass's own sons, willing to sign on to the president's plan, as evidenced by the relative ease with which Lincoln's chosen emissary, Kansas senator Samuel Pomeroy, recruited a first shipload of around five hundred Blacks.[14] Nonetheless, Lincoln's efforts failed to result in a single ship of Black emigrants leaving the United States because he was unable to overcome the strong opposition of Central American governments—and the objections of his own secretary of state.[15] On September 24, Lincoln was forced to suspend the Chiriquí project, which even his own administration had determined was little more than "a swindling speculation."[16] The core problem with colonization, however, as the *Chicago Tribune* correctly discerned, was one of scale, for even if a few shiploads of emigrants could have been arranged, the sheer number of Black Americans—totaling about one-eighth of the US population—"utterly forbid and render futile these measures save on the most limited scale."[17]

There is no question that Lincoln sincerely believed in colonization—and had done so from his earliest days in politics as a Whig who idolized Henry Clay, a founding member of the American Colonization Society and its president for more than a decade. But Lincoln's White House remarks to the Black delegation must also be understood as part of Lincoln's effort to prepare the country for his Emancipation Proclamation. He may have failed to persuade Blacks to leave the country—or even offered them a viable plan to emigrate—but the primary audience for his White House remarks was not Blacks—and certainly not the Black guests he had invited to the White House—but northern Whites, which is presumably why he wanted a stenographer present and why he stressed that the presence of Blacks in the United States was the reason for "our white men cutting one another's throats." Had Lincoln wished to persuade Blacks alone, Lincoln presumably could have hewn to the "arguments of black independence and racial self-determination long made by African American emigration advocates," as Pomeroy did in making his presidentially sanctioned appeal on behalf of the Chiriquí mission.[18]

If Lincoln's belief in colonization was genuine, his decision to elevate the cause in August 1862 was also tactical. Lincoln's goal was less to rid the country of Blacks than to persuade Whites, who had the "power to resist" (to use Richard Neustadt's phrase) his yet unannounced emancipation order, that colonization was viable. Lincoln was also signaling that he was "pre-eminently the white man's president," as Douglass famously described Lincoln in his speech years later at the dedication of the Emancipation Memorial in 1876. Black abolitionists who condemned Lincoln's August 14 remarks for "pandering to the mob spirit" were not wrong, but it was pandering in the service of the yet-to-be announced Emancipation Proclamation.[19]

Lincoln seems to have hoped that a colonization success, even on a small scale, would make his planned emancipation edict more popular or at least palatable. However, as historian Mark Neely suggests, there is little if any evidence that the president's efforts to raise the salience of colonization meaningfully altered "the terms of the debate" about emancipation. Everybody continued to assume that if Blacks were freed, they "would forever form a part of the United States and would have to be somehow accommodated." Lincoln's persuasive efforts had again come up well short.[20]

CHAPTER 5

"The Time Has Come Now"
The Preliminary Proclamation

On Saturday, September 13, a month after meeting with the Black delegation from DC, Lincoln played host to two White religious leaders from Chicago, who had come to deliver a petition calling on the president to free all of the nation's slaves. The nine-page "Memorial of all Christian Denominations" had been drawn up following a public meeting in Chicago earlier in the month. Lincoln spoke for over an hour with the two ministers, one a Methodist and the other a Congregationalist, who pressed their case that by emancipating the slaves Lincoln would be following God's will.[1]

For the two ministers, the matter was simple. "If the leader will but utter a trumpet call," they told Lincoln, "the nation will respond with patriotic ardor." They placed their faith in "the power of the right word from the right man to develop the latent fire and enthusiasm of the masses." An emancipation proclamation was guaranteed to "send a thrill through the entire North, firing every patriotic heart, giving the people a glorious principle for which to suffer and to fight." Even if it led to some "desertion of Border State troops," as Lincoln worried, "the increased spirit of the North would replace them two to one." And in any event, they insisted, "the sooner we know who are our enemies the better." By drawing a clear moral line between freedom and slavery and rejecting "half-way measures," an emancipation proclamation would put the North on the side of righteousness and the path to victory.[2]

Lincoln did not disagree that a president's words mattered, any more than he disputed that God's will mattered. Indeed, he said it was his "earnest desire to know the will of Providence." Nor did he question any longer that he had a constitutional right as commander in chief to "take any measure which may best subdue the enemy," that issue was now settled in his mind, as he had explained in his much-publicized reply to Horace Greeley at the end of August. Moreover, he conceded that slavery lay "at the root of the rebellion," although he also stressed that the North already possessed an "important principle to rally and unite the people," namely, the "fundamental idea" of democratic "constitutional government." But ascertaining the right course of action on such a fraught and tangled subject on which "good men do not agree" was not the simple moral calculus that the clergymen insisted. After all, he reminded them, devout religious leaders "with the most opposite opinions and advice" on the issue claimed with equal certainty "to represent the Divine will." To Lincoln, it seemed "quite possible that God's purpose is something different from the purpose of either party." In any event, since these were not "the days of miracles" and he could hardly "expect a direct revelation" of God's purposes, he could only "study the plain physical facts of the case" to "ascertain what is possible and learn what appears to be wise and right."[3]

Having admonished his guests for presuming that God's purposes were so easily divined, Lincoln assured them that the subject had been on his mind perpetually these past weeks and months, "by day and night, more than any other," and tried to explain some of the "difficulties" that had "thus far" prevented him from deciding to issue a proclamation of the sort they desired. For starters, he was reluctant "to issue a document that the whole world will see must necessarily be inoperative, like the Pope's bull against the comet!" What good would that do? How would *my word* free the slaves, when I cannot enforce the Constitution in the rebel states." Was there any "court, or magistrate, or individual" in the rebel states, he asked, "that would be influenced by it?"[4] Moreover, if the practical object was to induce slaves to flee their masters and deprive the South of essential labor, why would a presidential proclamation have any more effect than the Second Confiscation Act, "which offers protection and freedom to the slaves of rebel masters who come within our lines?" And even if a presidential proclamation would induce slaves en masse "to throw themselves upon us," how was the army to "feed and care for such a multitude"? Moreover, no presidential statement could prevent the South from "reducing the blacks to slavery again" if "the pressure of the war should call off our forces . . . to defend some other point." In short, an emancipation proclamation was not the panacea that the clergymen seemed to believe it was. Such an order might, on balance, prove to be the best course of action as a "practical war measure"—and Lincoln assured the two ministers that he had "not decided against such a proclamation"—but he could not, at the stroke of a pen, as the clergymen hoped, "leave our country free forever."[5]

The meeting with the Chicago clergymen came toward the end of a particularly difficult period for Lincoln and his administration. According to a September 16 diary entry by Secretary of the Navy Gideon Welles, Lincoln appeared "sadly perplexed and distressed by events," which had gone from bad to worse over the course of the summer. A dismal month of August ended with a devastating Union defeat at the Second Battle of Bull Run, after which, Lincoln later said, "things looked darker than ever." Attorney General Edwards Bates reported that the president "seemed wrung by the bitterest anguish [and] said he felt almost ready to hang himself." For the first time in the more than sixteen months of war, it appeared that the Confederate army might even be able to take Washington, DC, a prospect that looked even more alarming when Lee's army, for the first time, on September 4, crossed the Potomac into Maryland, only twenty-five miles from the nation's capital.[6]

So profound was Lincoln's concern for the capital's safety after the destruction of General John Pope's Army of Virginia that he returned full command of the army to General George McClellan, who he had sidelined in favor of Pope less than two months earlier after McClellan's bungled Peninsular Campaign. As much as Lincoln continued to distrust and dislike McClellan, and even while he suspected that McClellan and officers loyal to the general had deliberately refused to come to Pope's aid on the battlefield because they "wanted [Pope] to fail," he believed he was now left with no option but to pivot back to McClellan, even if it meant rewarding what he regarded as "unpardonable" and "shocking" behavior. McClellan might suffer from the "slows," but Lincoln believed he needed McClellan's abilities to "reorganize the army and bring it out of chaos." As important, Lincoln calculated that at this fraught moment of vulnerability he could ill afford to alienate the general who "has the army with him." For Lincoln, restoring McClellan's command was a humiliating capitulation—one he described as the "greatest trial and most painful duty of his official life."[7]

Pope's crushing defeat and the turn to McClellan fed a growing sentiment within the Washington community that Lincoln was not up to the job. "An unfavorable impression" of Lincoln and his administration "is getting abroad," Welles confided in his diary on September 17. Even many of those who liked Lincoln, who considered him honest, sensible, and intelligent, were concluding that he lacked "the decision and energy the country wants." Many Republicans worried that Lincoln did not have the fortitude and military experience to stand up to the likes of McClellan and feared he was being "bullied" by the generals. Some, including within his own administration, fretted that the president was without "administrative ability and experience," which, together with his "unsuspicious" nature, was allowing him to be manipulated by his imperious secretary of state, William Henry Seward. And as the military defeats mounted, many antislavery Republicans became increasingly exasperated with the president's failure to take more forceful action against slavery.[8]

It was against this backdrop of political weakness, a mounting drumbeat of criticism of his leadership, and what Mark Neely describes as a "temporary loss of political mastery" that Lincoln summoned his cabinet for a special meeting on Monday, September 22, to announce that he had decided that "the time has come now" to issue the Emancipation Proclamation. Before reading the proclamation to them, Lincoln admitted that he wished "it were a better time [and] that we were in a better condition" and recognized that he had "not so much of the confidence of the people as I had some time since," but he had decided that there was no putting it off anymore. The proclamation, as he told Edward Pierrepoint, was "my last card," the final roll of the dice.[9]

Lincoln's position of weakness is often missed by the conventional narrative, which tells the tale of a methodical and sagacious Lincoln waiting patiently for just the right moment to unveil the proclamation. It is true that Lincoln waited to announce the proclamation until after the Battle of Antietam, in which McClellan succeeded in driving

Lee's army back across the Potomac. In doing so, he appeared to follow Seward's advice in July to wait for a Union victory to roll out the proclamation. But after the "quasi-victory" at Antietam, the Union war effort was hardly going any better than it had been two months before when Seward and Weed persuaded Lincoln to "wait on events." The battle itself, in which both sides suffered heavy casualties, was "in effect a draw," despite McClellan's forces outnumbering Lee's two to one. The truth was that McClellan "managed the battle disastrously," and much to Lincoln's frustration failed to press his advantage and chase down the retreating Lee, even though he had thousands of fresh troops at his disposal. As Lincoln admitted to his cabinet, with delicate understatement: "The action of the army against the rebels has not been quite what I should have best liked."[10]

None of that mattered now though. Lincoln explained to the cabinet that several weeks back, while saying "nothing to any one," he had promised himself and his Maker that when Lee was driven out of Maryland he would at once issue a proclamation of emancipation "such as I thought most likely to be useful." God had granted the victory he so desperately sought, and now it was his "duty to move forward in the cause of emancipation." By framing his decision as a "solemn vow" or "covenant" with God, Lincoln made clear that the matter of the proclamation's timing or efficacy was no longer up for debate. He was happy to accept suggestions to improve the language in the document "or in any other minor matter," but that was all. "His mind was fixed—his decision made" in favor of the proclamation.[11]

The central thrust of the four-page proclamation he read to the cabinet was similar to the one he had drawn up in July, giving the Confederate states until January 1, 1863, to put down their arms or else their slaves would become "forever free."[12] At the same time, Lincoln's proclamation protected slavery in the border states, promising, as he had in the July draft, to recommend "upon the next meeting of Congress" a "practical measure" to compensate states loyal to the Union that voluntarily adopted the gradual or immediate abolishment of slavery." Moreover, despite the insurmountable difficulties encountered by the Chiriquí project and Lincoln's lack of success in persuading Blacks to embrace colonization, he added a pledge, which had not been in the

July draft, to continue "the effort to colonize persons of African descent, with their consent, upon this continent or elsewhere."[13]

There is no reason to doubt Lincoln's claim that he had promised himself and his God that he would issue the proclamation as soon as Lee withdrew back into Virginia.[14] But to take this explanation of his decision-making process at face value obscures the political context that circumscribed his options. The most important of these constraints was what is today called the Second Confiscation Act, but which at the time was often referred to as the Confiscation-Emancipation Act.[15] That act gave the rebels sixty days to give up their arms or face confiscation of all property. That sixty-day statutory deadline, which Lincoln had duly proclaimed in July, was set to expire on September 23, the day after Lincoln assembled his cabinet to read the proclamation. Lincoln had to issue some kind of order relating to the congressionally mandated forfeiture of property, as emancipation advocates reminded the president.[16]

Indeed, from the moment Lincoln signed the Second Confiscation Act into law, he was "bombarded with calls to issue the proclamation." Adding to the building pressure on the president in the late summer were leaks presumably emanating from his cabinet. Just days after Greeley published his "Prayer of Twenty Millions," which called on Lincoln to more zealously enforce the "emancipating provisions of the new Confiscation Act," Greeley's *New York Tribune* published a largely accurate story, based "on so many sources that it can no longer be considered a state secret," reporting that Lincoln had already drafted a proclamation of emancipation "two or three weeks ago" but had shelved it because of opposition from Seward and Blair. That others had insider knowledge of the July 22nd cabinet meeting was evident from the *Chicago Tribune*'s confident pronouncement on August 27: "From the tenor of [Lincoln's] remarks" in his reply to Greeley, "if the next battle in Virginia results in a decided victory for our army" the president will "forthwith" issue a proclamation of emancipation.[17]

Not everyone in the cabinet was persuaded that Lee's retreat made this an opportune time for a proclamation of emancipation. Postmaster General Montgomery Blair favored emancipation in principle, but he thought it unwise to issue the proclamation just weeks before the fall elections. He warned Lincoln that an emancipation proclamation would weaken "the patriotic element" in the border states and could lead those states to secede. He also worried that it would give Democratic partisans throughout the North "a club . . . to beat the Administration" and thereby "endanger our power in Congress, and put the power in the next House of Representatives in the hands of those opposed to the war, or to our mode of carrying it on." An emancipation proclamation that led to the Democratic Party taking control of Congress could end up undermining the war effort and emancipation.[18]

Lincoln acknowledged the force of Blair's first objection relating to the effect on the border states. He had relied on the same argument just days earlier with the Chicago clergymen, and his concern about the border states' reactions had been a crucial part of why he had backed away from issuing the proclamation in July. But after trying in vain, month after month, to persuade the border states to adopt his preferred plan of gradual, compensated emancipation, Lincoln's patience had run out. Although he considered Blair's objection to be "undoubtedly serious," the dangers of inaction, in his mind, now outweighed the risks of action. As for Blair's other argument about the political effects of the proclamation in the North, Lincoln brushed it aside as having "not much weight with him" since "their clubs would be used against us, take what course we might."[19]

Although Lincoln dismissed Blair's warning about the upcoming elections, he remained profoundly unsure whether "the people had been quite educated up to" acceptance of the proclamation, a feeling of uncertainty shared by others in the cabinet, even those who heartily approved the proclamation.[20] Indeed, that was rather the point of Lincoln's talk of having made a solemn pact with God since it enabled him to sidestep those difficult questions that had held him back in July—namely, whether "the people were with him" on the proclamation and whether it "could be made effective."[21]

While his covenant with God may have helped Lincoln act in the face of continuing uncertainty about the proclamation's public support as well as its efficacy,[22] it should not obscure the meticulous attention Lincoln paid to how his unilateral directive would be received by the public and by political elites. In this respect, Welles's approving characterization of the proclamation as "a despotic act in the cause of the Union . . .

and . . . of freedom" is as misleading as the "dictatorial" charges that were leveled against the proclamation by Lincoln's critics.[23]

For starters, while Lincoln began the proclamation by invoking his unilateral authority as "President of the United States, and Commander-in-chief of the Army and Navy," he was careful also to ground the authority for his proclamation in congressional legislation, specifically "an act to make an additional Article of War," passed in March 1862, which prohibited anyone in the military from returning fugitive slaves, and "an Act to suppress Insurrection to punish Treason and Rebellion" (aka the Second Confiscation Act), enacted in July. Indeed, half of the president's one thousand-word proclamation was taken up with invoking congressional authority and quoting from the text of the relevant sections of these two laws. Lincoln did not claim to be acting alone but in accordance with congressional wishes.[24]

And even while he framed the proclamation to his cabinet as a fait accompli for which he alone bore ultimate responsibility, he in fact reached his decision only after carefully canvassing his cabinet members, individually and collectively. The cabinet's supportive response showed that Lincoln had done the political work necessary to secure the buy-in from the cabinet that had been missing in July. Salmon Chase, for instance, while acknowledging that the proclamation did not "mark out exactly the course I should myself prefer," told Lincoln that it "fully satisfies me that you have given to every proposition which has been made, a kind and candid consideration," and that as a result he was "ready to take it just as written, and to stand by it with all my heart." And while Blair remained unpersuaded that the time was right for issuing the proclamation, he promised the president that he would "make no objection to issuing the Proclamation." Lincoln was able to issue the proclamation because his politically diverse cabinet was willing to support it, something that had not been true in July.[25]

Lincoln acted on his conviction that public opinion in the United States was "everything" and that a proclamation without public backing would be ineffective. His August 23rd public reply to Greeley, in which he declared that his "paramount object" was to save the Union, was an effort to insulate the proclamation from criticism that it changed the purpose of the war from a war for the Union to a war against slavery.[26]

His audience was not abolitionists and strongly antislavery Republicans like Greeley, who he knew would embrace the proclamation, even if they groused about its tardiness, but rather more conservative elements, including those within his own party, who resisted the notion of a war of emancipation. That is why Lincoln chose to publish his reply not in Greeley's *Tribune* but in Washington's *National Intelligencer*, a conservative Unionist paper that backed Tennessee's John Bell and the Constitutional Union Party in 1860 and remained "decidedly unfriendly to the idea of emancipation."[27]

How effective Lincoln's reply to Greeley was in shaping public opinion is difficult to determine with precision. There were those like Thurlow Weed, who had helped persuade Lincoln not to issue the proclamation in July, who welcomed the letter for giving the party "ground to stand on" and for undercutting the "the ultras" who he believed had been pressuring the president into a "false position." And there were others, such as Missouri's Unionist senator John Henderson, who saw in Lincoln's letter a recognition that "emancipation proclamations can only serve to make things worse." Pro-emancipation advocates were also divided, with reactions ranging from abolitionist Wendell Phillips's savage denunciation of Lincoln's reply as "the most disgraceful document that ever came from the head of a free people" to Sydney Gay's confident pronouncement that the reply appeared to signal the president's imminent intention "to announce that the destruction of Slavery is the price of our salvation."[28]

Given the "Delphic qualities" of Lincoln's reply, which "allowed different people to read very different messages into it," there seems reason to doubt the reply's effectiveness in preparing the nation for the proclamation.[29] Certainly his remarks to the Chicago clergymen were hardly likely to have increased support for the proclamation since his comments were mostly a series of arguments against the value of issuing a proclamation, which meant, as Mark Neely points out, that newspaper readers saw Lincoln's proclamation on the 22nd and the following day (when his comments to the clergymen were published in the newspapers) could read the president explaining why a proclamation would be futile or counterproductive. Even less helpful in preparing people for the proclamation was the publication of his poorly received comments about the virtues of colonization, which appear only to have succeeded, as James Oakes notes, "in heightening the speculation as to whether he intended to issue an emancipation proclamation."[30]

In all likelihood, Lincoln's own words between July and September had little effect on public opinion regarding emancipation. What was gradually "converting hundreds of thousands of moderate and conservative peace-loving men" to emancipation, as Robert Dale Owen surmised, was the war itself. And ironically, in view of Seward's counsel and Lincoln's determination to wait on a victory, the Union's defeats were ultimately more important than any victory in preparing the ground for the Emancipation Proclamation. The worse the Union army did and the longer the war dragged on, the more people became receptive to the argument that emancipation, by depriving the South of the labor force on which its economy depended, was the only way to defeat the Confederates. An argument from military necessity, which Lincoln offered in both his reply to Greeley and to the Chicago clergymen, worked best if existing policies were proving insufficient to win the war.[31]

One need not accept Neely's contention that Lincoln bungled virtually every aspect of the public rollout of the proclamation, "confusing the public, not preparing it," to recognize that Lincoln was hardly the commanding, masterful figure of legend.[32] When Lincoln famously said, "I claim not to have controlled events, but confess plainly that events have controlled me," he was not offering up false modesty but hard-earned wisdom about the limits on presidential leadership. What stands out about the two months leading up to the proclamation is not Lincoln's blundering or his wizardry in shaping public opinion but rather the weakness of both his office and his political position. The proclamation did not free Lincoln from the constraints on presidential power. On the contrary, it dramatically underscored Richard Neustadt's thesis about the "limits upon presidential 'powers.'"[33]

CHAPTER 6

The Cost of Command
The Fall Elections

Lincoln's proclamation is reported to have "electrified" the country. Reactions, of course, were wildly divergent. Those opposed to the decree assailed it for enticing slaves to murder their masters, violating the Constitution, and sacrificing the Union "upon the bloody altar of fanatical Abolitionism." Some critics predicted that it would lead Union soldiers to lay down their arms rather than fight for "an Abolition war." Some opponents saw in the decree the work of a tyrant or dictator; others said it showed a weak president bending to the will of radical abolitionists. Even some who had long desired the president to endorse emancipation complained that the proclamation's style was too "dry" and that it lacked an "expression of sound moral feeling against Slavery." More than a few abolitionists complained about its tardiness.[1]

However, most Republicans greeted the proclamation with enthusiasm and many hailed it as a defining event in the life of the nation. The *Philadelphia Press* likened it to a "second Declaration of Independence from slavery." A Massachusetts paper wrote that Lincoln had "written his name in history in letters of light" by producing a document that "marks an epoch in the history of this nation and the world." The *New York Times* agreed that there had never been a "more far reaching document since the foundation of this government." Even Karl Marx, an authority on momentous manifestos, thought that despite its appearance as a "routine summons sent by a lawyer to the lawyer of the opposing party," Lincoln's "manifesto abolishing slavery [was] the most important document in American history since the establishment of the Union, tantamount to the tearing up of the old American Constitution."[2]

Although appreciative of the praise lavished upon him (and of course well aware of the criticisms), Lincoln was more circumspect in his assessment of the order. When Vice President Hannibal Hamlin gushed that the president's proclamation "will stand as the great act of the age," Lincoln wrote back that while he "hoped something from the proclamation," his "expectations are not as sanguine as are those of some friends." The order was but "six days old" and while the "commendation in newspapers and by distinguished individuals is all that a vain man could wish," Lincoln noted that "stocks have declined, and troops have come forward more slowly than ever." Looked "soberly in the face," these results were "not very satisfactory." A week after the proclamation, the army had "fewer troops in the field" than it did before the order's announcement. The North had responded to the proclamation "sufficiently in breath," Lincoln closed, "but breath alone kills no rebels."[3]

Lincoln's somber assessment may have been shaped by reports that reached the president suggesting that the proclamation was fueling discontent among army officers, especially those close to General George McClellan. The day before writing to Hamlin, Lincoln had summoned to his office Major John J. Key, the brother of a McClellan confidant regarded by some as the general's "evil genius." Major Key had allegedly told a fellow officer that the Army of the Potomac's true objective was not to destroy the Confederate army but rather to battle to a stalemate so as to "make a compromise and save slavery." Under Lincoln's questioning, Key insisted on his fidelity to the Union but did not deny making the claim that "the only way the Union could be preserved" was if the two sides "come together fraternally, and slavery be saved." Fearful that such "staff talk" could spread, Lincoln made "an example" of the major by promptly dismissing him from the Union army and then having White House aide John Hay "disseminate a news item publicizing and justifying the dismissal."[4]

Although Lincoln downplayed concerns that such talk revealed a "McClellan conspiracy," he was sufficiently worried that he decided to visit McClellan at Harpers Ferry "to satisfy himself personally . . . of the purposes[,] intentions and fidelity of McClellan, his officers, and the army." Lincoln was right to worry about how the proclamation, a military order, would be received by the military officers, particularly McClellan, who would be responsible for executing and even communicating it. On September 25, two days before Lincoln met with Key, General McClellan confided to his wife that he was considering resigning his commission rather than carry out the president's order. "I cannot make up my mind," he declared, "to fight for such an accursed doctrine as that of servile insurrection." He made his disapproval even clearer in a letter the following day to a prominent New York Democrat, William Aspinwall, in which he characterized the Emancipation Proclamation as "inaugurating servile war" and lambasted Lincoln's order suspending habeas corpus, which was issued on September 24, for "changing our free institutions into a despotism" with "one stroke of the pen."⁵

McClellan canvassed an array of associates, including other generals, about their opinions of the Emancipation Proclamation and what they thought he should do. Speaking with three leading generals whom he had invited for a "camp dinner" in his tent, McClellan revealed that he had been urged by both leading politicians and high-ranking "army officers... near to him... to put himself in open opposition" to the order, an order that McClellan "attributed to radical influences at Washington." The three generals advised him in unequivocal terms that publicly criticizing the president's policy "would be properly regarded as a usurpation" and would be a "fatal error." Aspinall offered McClellan the same advice that he should submit "quietly" to the president's proclamation.⁶

When the president visited McClellan in early October, the general still had not communicated anything to the Army of the Potomac regarding the president's order. Not until October 7, two weeks after the president's proclamation was issued (and two days after Lincoln had returned to the nation's capital), did McClellan finally issue a General Order directing "the attention of officers and soldiers of the army of the Potomac" to the president's proclamation. However, McClellan could not resist adding his own commentary to the president's order in which he reaffirmed the necessity of "strict subordination" of the military to the policy set by civil authorities, while also noting that "the remedy for political errors, if any are committed, is to be found only in the action of the people at the polls." McClellan's defenders insisted that his communiqué was only acknowledging the "agitation in camp on the subject" and making clear that whatever strong feelings soldiers might have about the president's proclamation they were duty-bound to follow the presidential directive. However, McClellan was also, at a minimum, signaling his own misgivings about the proclamation. And with the fall elections in crucial states only a few weeks away, his commentary could easily be read as a call to vote against Lincoln's Republican Party.[7]

Just as McClellan recognized that he could not afford to openly defy the president no matter how much he despised the "Gorilla" and his policies, so Lincoln calculated that he could not afford to dismiss his general despite the insubordination and recalcitrance. Lincoln's formal constitutional powers were one thing, his actual power over McClellan quite another. In part, Lincoln held off firing McClellan because he wasn't sure who he could put in the general's place "who would do better," but the more important factor staying the president's hand was the looming fall elections. Firing the victorious general who had just driven Lee's army out of Maryland and secured the safety of the nation's capital was not a risk the president was prepared to take as voters throughout the North were about to go to the polls (Lincoln ultimately fired McClellan on Wednesday, November 5th, the day after the last vote was cast in the fall congressional elections).[8]

In the mid-nineteenth century, congressional elections were not held on a single day, as is the case today.[9] Two northern states had already held their congressional elections: Oregon, which went to the polls in June, and Maine, which held elections in early September. Eight others, principally border states and northeastern states, would not select congressional representatives until the following year, on dates ranging from March to November. However, a majority of northern states, including the six most populous, held their congressional elections in either October or November, with the pivotal states of Indiana, Ohio, and Pennsylvania voting in mid-October and Illinois, New Jersey, and New York among the ten states to hold elections in the first week of November. All told, almost 80 percent of the US House's seats would be selected between October 14 and November 4.[10]

The few congressional elections held prior to the Emancipation Proclamation had been basically a wash, with Republicans flipping a congressional seat and the governor's house in Oregon in June and losing a congressional seat while retaining the governorship (albeit with a reduced vote share) in Maine. But as historian Allen Guelzo notes, the president's proclamation "breathed new and toxic life back into the Northern Democrats," especially in the middle swath of the country stretching from Illinois to New York. The president's proclamation suspending the writ of habeas corpus and declaring martial law only helped to amplify opposition alarms about Lincoln's supposedly "despotic rule."[11]

On the evening Lincoln returned to the capital after his meeting with McClellan, Indiana governor Oliver Morton huddled with Treasury Secretary Salmon Chase to express his fears that Republicans appeared to be heading to a disastrous defeat in his state's congressional elections. The week before, Chase heard similar forebodings of defeat in Ohio from Senator John Sherman, who warned of a newly energized Democratic Party in the state "working with wonderful activity & hope of success" in contrast to the "inert" and demoralized Republican Party. Without a change in fortune, Sherman predicted, the administration "will be in the minority" in the next Congress.[12]

The October election results were every bit as bad as forecast. In Indiana, a state Lincoln had won by almost nine points in 1860, the Republicans' 7-4 House advantage flipped to a 7-4 Democratic advantage, and Democrats also captured control of the state house, which would enable them to appoint a new US senator in January. In Pennsylvania, which Lincoln had carried with 56 percent of the vote, the overwhelming Republican 19-6 advantage in the House of Representatives gave way to an evenly balanced congressional delegation. Among the Pennsylvania Republicans to lose their seats was the strongly antislavery Speaker of the House, Galusha Grow. It was the same grim story in Ohio, another state Lincoln had carried comfortably in 1860, where the Republican share of congressional seats dropped from over 60 percent to closer to a quarter of the seats. All told, in the three states, Democrats picked up sixteen House seats while Republicans lost nineteen (reapportionment had led to a net loss of three seats in these states), disastrous losses that left everyone around the president feeling "all blue," reported John Nicolay.[13]

Things were not much more encouraging in the elections three weeks later, particularly in Lincoln's home state of Illinois, where Democrats won nine of fourteen House seats. Among the Republicans to lose their bid for a House seat was one of Lincoln's closest friends and a vigorous defender of the Emancipation Proclamation, Leonard Swett; adding insult to injury, the district Swett was running in included Lincoln's hometown of Springfield. The Democrats also flipped control of both houses of the state legislature, which meant that come January the Democrats would be able to oust Lincoln's confidant Orville Browning (who had been selected to finish out Stephen Douglas's US Senate term) and replace him with a Democrat. One of the new state legislature's first acts in January was to pass a resolution condemning the Emancipation Proclamation as "a gigantic usurpation, . . . converting the war . . . into the crusade for the sudden, unconditional, and violent liberation of 3,000,000 negro slaves," an act that would usher in a social "revolution" that "cannot be contemplated without the most dismal foreboding of horror and dismay."[14]

In Delaware, Lincoln suffered the humiliation of having his ally George Fisher lose his House seat. Fisher was in "no doubt . . . his support for compensated emancipation had cost him the election." Certainly, Democrats made Fisher's support of Lincoln's "ridiculous compensated emancipation scheme" a centerpiece of their campaign, accusing Fisher of having shown a "compassion for the negro slaves of Delaware [that] led him to exhibit an entire want of compassion for the poor white laboring population."[15]

The anti-administration current also ran strongly in New Jersey, where the Democrats won four of the five House seats (a pickup of one) and flipped control of the state house and the governorship. However, it was the results in neighboring New York that were perhaps the biggest disappointment to the administration. Republicans went from having a thirteen-seat advantage in the nation's largest congressional delegation to a three-seat deficit. Among those swept into Congress was the secessionist sympathizer Fernando Wood, who as mayor of New York City had been a continual thorn in Lincoln's side. Most alarming was the result of the closely watched governor's race, in which the unabashedly pro-emancipation Republican James Wadsworth was defeated by the outspoken conservative Democrat Horatio Seymour, who upon accepting his party's nomination on September 10 had thrown down the gauntlet to the "fanatical majority" of radical Republicans in Congress. Seymour singled out for criticism the Second Confiscation Act, saving his most lurid rhetoric for the provision calling for the arming of slaves, which he said was a "proposal for the butchery of women and children, for scenes of lust and rapine, of arson and murder unparalleled in the history of the world."[16]

Obviously, the shifting electoral tide was not all or even mostly down to the Emancipation Proclamation. A generalized frustration at what Lincoln called "the ill-success of the war" undoubtedly helped to propel the Democrats' resurgence. There were also state-specific and district-specific events that shaped the outcomes. In Pennsylvania, for instance, Republicans were likely hurt by Confederate general J. E. B. Stuart's daring end run around McClellan just days before the election that resulted in his troops occupying the town of Chambersburg for a day and "cutting telegraph lines, seizing horses, and demolishing railroad machine shops, a depot, and several trains" in the vicinity before returning unscathed to Virginia just two days before the state's voters went to the polls.[17]

If it would be a mistake to lay all of the blame for the disastrous midterm election results on the Emancipation Proclamation, it would be equally wrong to downplay let alone dismiss its effect on the elections, as a defensive Lincoln was prone to do in the immediate wake of the election. Like many on the losing end of an electoral contest, Lincoln blamed defeat on the press for "vilifying and disparaging the administration." He also faulted Democrats for being "determined to re-instate themselves in power," as if the opposition party trying to win an election was somehow a surprise. And like many Republicans, he dismissed the party's heavy defeat as largely an artificial product of soldiers' inability to vote; with "our friends going to war," Lincoln explained to Carl Schurz on November 10, the Democrats "were left in a majority."[18]

The reality was far more complex, as Lincoln surely recognized. In Lincoln's home state of Illinois, Republican fortunes were affected by secretary of war Edwin Stanton's directive, issued only a few days before Lincoln's proclamation, to resettle former slaves being held in the military's "contraband camp" in the southern Illinois town of Cairo.[19]

The northward migration of Blacks that Stanton's order initiated was portrayed by Democrats as "the beginning of the results we may expect from the emancipation policy"—namely, the "Africanization" of the state. Reflecting on his surprise defeat, Swett was in no doubt, as he told his law partner, that "the Proclamation hurt rather than helped us. Negroes from the south were taken into our state. Fifty or more went to Livingston. This did great harm."[20] His strongly antislavery partner didn't need any convincing that "infernal negro immigration into Illinois" had been a "terrible stroke" that doomed Swett's chances. Voters might support emancipation as a general principle or as a military necessity, but the results in Illinois showed that support could evaporate if voters thought it meant living side by side with Blacks.

In the New York gubernatorial race, where the two candidates were separated by fewer than eleven thousand voters out of over three hundred thousand votes cast (and where the turnout rate was unchanged from where it had been—79 percent—in the previous 1858 gubernatorial election), the Emancipation Proclamation almost certainly played a pivotal role. Writing to his sister just days before Lincoln unveiled the Emancipation Proclamation, Seymour confided that his election was "not probable" but that he had got into the race because he felt "a sharp bitter fight" was essential to rebuild an opposition party. But Lincoln's proclamation emancipating the slaves (as well his proclamation suspending habeas corpus) injected fresh life into Seymour's campaign. Instead of remaining in a defensive crouch fending off charges of disloyalty, Seymour and his Democratic supporters were able to go on the attack against a proclamation that they insisted was unconstitutional, a threat to the White workers everywhere, a "barbarous" invitation to "servile war," and that divided the people of the North while unifying and strengthening the South.[21]

New York's Republicans, too, contributed to keeping the Emancipation Proclamation at the forefront of the campaign. When the party assembled to select their gubernatorial nominee just two days after the president issued the proclamation, the delegates picked the unabashedly pro-emancipation candidate backed by Horace Greeley over a War Democrat and emancipation skeptic backed by Thurlow Weed, who remained every bit as apprehensive about the political effects of the

Emancipation Proclamation as he was back in July when he had helped Seward talk Lincoln out of issuing the proclamation. The treacherous politics surrounding the Emancipation Proclamation were evident from the way that Wadsworth framed his support of the proclamation in his acceptance speech. Emancipated slaves, he assured New Yorkers, would never come north to compete with White workers, and he predicted that even those free Blacks currently residing in the North would inevitably "drift to the South where they will find a congenial climate and vast tracts of land." Emancipation was a good and noble thing but only because it could be achieved without White New Yorkers having to live with Blacks. Freed slaves would be the South's problem.[22]

Wadsworth's assurances, like Lincoln's colonization plan, failed to blunt Democratic attacks on the proclamation that exploited fears about emancipation leading to Blacks migrating north and taking the jobs of Whites. The drawn-out war may have increased popular support for emancipation as a military necessity, but voters' attitudes on slavery and race were complex and highly susceptible to elite framing—and Democrats in the campaign were relentless in inducing voters to think about emancipation in terms of the threat posed by "a swarthy inundation of negro laborers and paupers."[23] Moreover, the Emancipation Proclamation helped Democrats shift voters' attention away from questions about disloyalty and war, where Democrats were invariably on the defensive, and toward an issue that galvanized its own partisans and divided and discomforted the administration's supporters. Lincoln's protestations notwithstanding, the Emancipation Proclamation was bad politics that, as Swett surmised, generally did more harm than good.[24]

Lincoln's unilateral proclamation had come at a high political cost. The congressional elections in October and November saw Democrats pick up thirty-three seats while Republicans lost twenty-four seats (reapportionment added nine seats in the fourteen states that voted in the six weeks following the proclamation). Despite controlling nearly 60 percent of the House seats in the 37th Congress, Republican losses in the North were so heavy, particularly in Ohio, Pennsylvania, and New York, that there was no chance that they would have a majority in the new 38th Congress. Instead, to retain the Speaker's gavel, they would need to rely on a coalition with border state representatives from the Unconditional Union Party, which made the following year's elections in the three border states of Kentucky, Maryland, and West Virginia of critical importance. Whether the 38th Congress would back emancipation was very much in question, although fortunately for Lincoln the new Congress would not be sworn in until the end of 1863.[25]

Allen Guelzo suggests that because "the timing of the Proclamation amounted to political suicide," it shows "how adamant Lincoln was about emancipation." It might be more accurate, however, to say that it reveals how much Lincoln misjudged the politics of emancipation. Admittedly, to his credit, Lincoln never put much credence in extravagant predictions about the proclamation's magical qualities for rallying the North. He never saw the directive as the silver bullet that many antislavery advocates did. However, he had expected that it "would help somewhat at the North" and that those effects would be "instantaneous." And he had cavalierly brushed aside warnings that it would hurt the administration in the upcoming elections.[26]

Whatever the precise electoral effects of the proclamation, Democrats were convinced that the election results were a repudiation of Lincoln's unilateral directive—and a clear sign that the people of the North wanted a war to restore the Union, not a fight to abolish slavery. Democrats were emboldened by their stunning success at the polls, not only to attack the proclamation but increasingly Lincoln himself. Many Democrats were even convinced that the election meant that the president would have to back down on his pledge to issue the final proclamation on January 1st. More than a few Republicans also fretted that a chastened Lincoln would retreat from the proclamation.[27]

Indeed, as the extent of the Republican Party's electoral reverses became clear, Lincoln expressed concerns that he had badly misjudged the politics of emancipation, telling "at least six persons," according to one report, that the preliminary proclamation might have been "the great mistake of his life." Asked about the truth of this remark, Lincoln is said to have replied that "he had put himself into a minority with the people, and he well knew that it was impossible for him to carry on a great war against the feelings of the majority of the people."[28]

As members of both parties returned to Washington for the lame duck session of the 37th Congress that convened on December 1, they faced a president whose popularity in the country and "professional reputation" among the Washington community had reached a low ebb, ruthlessly exposing the high cost of command and the fundamental weakness of the American presidency.[29]

CHAPTER 7

On Deaf Ears
Lincoln's Final "Olive Branch"

Presidents today deliver the State of the Union message in person to a joint session of Congress in a made-for-television spectacle replete with primetime pomp and pageantry, punctuated by "unending waves of applause." In the nineteenth century, however, the president's annual message, as it was then called, was an altogether more subdued albeit no less ritualized event.[1]

Upon being called to order at noon on December 1, 1862, the 37th Congress dispatched a committee to inform the president that it was ready to "receive any communication which [the president] might wish to make." The six-person congressional delegation then made its way down the mile-long stretch of Pennsylvania Avenue that connected the US Capitol and the president's house, delivered its invitation, and returned to the Capitol with the news that the president was prepared to transmit his annual message. Shortly thereafter, at about 1:30 p.m., Lincoln's private secretary John Nicolay arrived on Capitol Hill to deliver copies of the message to the House and to the Senate. The clerk of each body was then tasked with reading the president's message to the respective body's legislators.[2]

If the members of Congress expected Lincoln would use his message to clarify his intentions about the final proclamation, they were to be sorely disappointed. Instead, Lincoln's message doubled down on his oft-rejected plan of compensated emancipation, making only glancing reference to the Emancipation Proclamation and only then as a segue to elaborate on his pledge in the preliminary proclamation to recommend to Congress a "practical measure" for compensated emancipation. As Lincoln's close friend and former campaign manager David Davis attested, "Mr. Lincoln's whole soul is absorbed in his plan of remunerative emancipation and he thinks if Congress don't fail him that the problem is solved."[3]

Unlike in his message to Congress in March 1862, however, Lincoln now offered his plan in the form not of statutory changes but of three constitutional amendments. By framing the proposal as constitutional amendments, which would require the approval not only of Congress but of three-fourths of the states, including "necessarily... seven of the slave States," Lincoln signaled that his final "olive branch," unlike his March message to Congress, was intended not only for the border states but for states that had joined the Confederacy as well.[4]

Lincoln's first amendment pledged compensation for slaveholders in any slave state that abolished slavery before 1900—an even more forgiving schedule than he had offered earlier in the year. The second promised compensation for any slave freed "by the chances of the war" so long as the slaveholder had not been "disloyal" during the "rebellion." And the final proposed amendment authorized Congress to "appropriate money, and otherwise provide, for colonizing free colored persons, with their own consent, at any place or places within the United States."[5]

Lincoln proceeded to defend the proposed articles "at some length"—a defense that was sufficiently long, he felt the need to beg Congress's "indulgence." Lincoln recognized the "great diversity" of views about slavery and "the African race" and offered his three amendments as a "compromise among the friends... of the Union" that embodied "a plan of... mutual concessions." Allowing thirty-seven years for emancipation would disappoint those on both sides of the debate over slavery, but Lincoln insisted that "the time spares both races from the evils of sudden derangement—in fact from the necessity of any derangement," particularly since "those whose habitual course of thought will be disturbed by the measure will have passed away before its consummation." As for "the now living slaves," they would be saved from "the vagrant destitution which must largely attend immediate emancipation in localities where their numbers are very great," and they would have the "inspiring assurance that their posterity shall be forever free."[6]

As to why those in the North should compensate those in the South for their slaves, Lincoln explained that "in a certain sense the liberation of slaves is the destruction of property." Moreover, he reminded Congress that "the people of the south are not more responsible for the original introduction of this property, than are the people of the north." Nor should the South necessarily be held more responsible for its continuance given that Americans in both regions "use cotton and sugar, and share the profits of dealing in them." Since all Americans are implicated in slavery, it was just that all bear the burden of financing its end.[7]

As he did in March, he rehearsed how much more "economical" compensated emancipation was than war. Lincoln added that his scheme had the added advantage that while the war "requires large sums, and requires them at once," gradual emancipation spread over almost four decades would make the financing even of large sums far more manageable, especially considering how much the country would expand in wealth and population over that time. Crucially, Lincoln argued, his proposal would not only "shorten the war" but "perpetuate the peace," since only by removing slavery could "the only great element of national discord" between North and South be permanently removed.[8]

Lincoln had little to say about the second article beyond observing that it would be "impracticable" to return to slavery those slaves freed as a result of the war. But since "in a property sense" some of them "belong to loyal owners," those slaveowners deserved the same compensation offered in the first amendment.[9]

As for the third amendment, he emphasized that it would not require Congress to fund colonization but only authorize Congress to do so. The amendment, he said, should be unobjectionable since it rested on "mutual consent" of both the people to be "deported" and those who would fund the deportation. Lincoln underlined that "I cannot make it better known than it already is, that I strongly favor colonization." But he also sought to dispel an objection to Blacks remaining in the country that was "largely imaginary, if not sometimes malicious." To those who said that if slaves were freed, Black laborers would replace White laborers, Lincoln exposed the illogic of the position. The amount of labor to be performed would not change, and once freed from compulsory work, Blacks, he insisted, would likely, at least for a time, work less than they had when they were enslaved, leading to *more* demand for White labor and higher wages. Moreover, "with deportation, even to a limited extent, enhanced wages to white labor is mathematically certain." For Lincoln this was a matter of basic economics: "Reduce the supply of black labor, by colonizing the black laborer out of the country, and, by precisely so much, you increase the demand for, and wages of, white labor."[10]

What about the "dreaded" fear that emancipation would mean that "freed people will swarm forth, and cover the whole land"? Emancipation, he pointed out, would not make Blacks more numerous, and even "equally distributed among the whites of the whole country . . . there would be but one colored to seven whites." "Could the one," Lincoln asked, "greatly disturb the seven?" He noted that there were "many communities now," including the District of Columbia, that had "more than one free colored person, to seven whites" without "any apparent consciousness of evil from it." Moreover, there was no reason to think that once emancipated, freed slaves would head north. When slavery was abolished in the nation's capital in April, Lincoln pointed out, there was no "irruption of colored people northward." Lincoln argued that "if gradual emancipation and deportation be adopted," freed slaves would have neither bondage nor destitution to flee from anymore. They would most likely continue to work for wages for their "old masters," at least until "new homes can be found for them, in congenial climes and with people of their own blood and race." Moreover, Lincoln pointed out, the northern states were free to decide for themselves whether "to receive" Blacks. In short, the North had nothing to fear from emancipation, especially if it was linked with a modest amount of colonization.[11]

Lincoln made it clear that in recommending compensated emancipation and colonization he was not signaling an intent to walk back the Emancipation Proclamation. But he also said that if his plan was adopted in a "timely" fashion—presumably before January 1, 1863, when the proclamation would go into effect—that would secure the "restoration of national authority" and thus remove the need for both the war and the proclamation. Adopting his compromise plan would "end the struggle now, and save the Union forever." The now-famous lines toward the close of the message—"The dogmas of the quiet past, are inadequate to the stormy present. . . . As our case is new, we must think anew, and act anew"—pleaded for the country to accept a compromise built around gradual, compensated emancipation and, if possible, voluntary colonization.[12]

The concluding paragraph offered some of Lincoln's most affecting rhetoric, including several of his most quotable lines: "The fiery trial through which we pass, will light us down, in honor or dishonor, to the latest generation," and "We shall nobly save, or meanly lose, the last best, hope of earth." Congress, however, seemed unmoved by Lincoln's rousing prose and by the plan he proposed. As Allen Guelzo notes, "There is little evidence that Lincoln's appeal won over anyone in Congress," least of all the border states.[13]

There was hardly more appetite for his compensated gradual emancipation plan than there had been when he first pitched it to Congress at the outset of the year. Lincoln's by-now-familiar litany of ideas—gradual emancipation, compensation for slaveholders, and colonization—seemed ill-suited to the urgency of the moment. Ohio senator William P. Cutler, a Republican, confided to his diary that Lincoln's plan of compensated emancipation was "a most impracticable scheme" that "nobody likes." Some could only laugh at the "astounding scheme." Even Browning could not fathom "the hallucination the President seems to be laboring under that Congress can suppress the rebellion by adopting his plan of compensated emancipation," a plan that would require "at least four years to have it adopted as he proposes." Frederick Douglass thought it showed the president was "demented." Others, like Massachusetts congressman Henry Dawes, said it made Lincoln seem hopelessly ineffectual and out of touch: "Whether the Republic shall live six months or not is the question thundering in our ears and the chief magistrate answers I've got a plan which is going to work well in the next century." Despite the president's lofty rhetoric, his carefully crafted arguments, and countless meetings and conversations, he once again failed to persuade Congress to follow his lead.[14]

Why did Lincoln use his December message to push a plan that had almost no chance of being adopted by Congress let alone by the requisite number of states? Why urge Americans to move beyond the "dogmas" of the past only to continue to cling so visibly to ideas that had been so often rejected in the past?[15] Granted Lincoln had received some reassuring signals in the fall that suggested that some of the border states, particularly Missouri, might be open to reconsidering their position on compensated emancipation.[16] And so deep was Lincoln's conviction that gradual emancipation with compensation to slaveholders was the best policy that he was prone to wishful thinking on the subject. However, even if Lincoln still believed, as Davis attested, that "if Congress will pass a Law authorizing the issuance of bonds for the payment of the emancipated negroes in the border states that Delaware, Maryland, Kentucky & Mo will accept the terms," that still leaves unanswered why Lincoln proposed a series of constitutional amendments rather than merely reupping his call for Congress to authorize compensation for slaveowners.[17]

One possible explanation for Lincoln's preference for constitutional amendments might be Lincoln's nervousness about what the federal courts would do.[18] But while Lincoln had good reason to worry that the Emancipation Proclamation could be vulnerable to legal challenge, particularly once the war was over,[19] Congress's power to appropriate monies to compensate slaveowners or to promote voluntary colonization did not face the same legal risks. And since there was virtually no prospect of these amendments being approved, it seems unlikely that Lincoln was motivated by a concern with the judiciary.

Perhaps Lincoln hoped that by packaging familiar ideas in the form of constitutional amendments the plan would not be easily dismissed as more of the same. And by proposing constitutional amendments instead of mere statutes, Lincoln may have been trying to elevate his plan of mutual concessions into a grand bargain, akin to a constitutional accord or settlement. The message may also have been intended to prepare the ground for the forthcoming proclamation by positioning Lincoln as the reluctant emancipator, whose actions were being forced on him by the unwillingness of others to accept reasonable compromises. He may even, as historian Michael Burlingame speculates, have wanted to "appear magnanimous by demonstrating his willingness to go to great lengths in helping [the border states] avoid the shock of sudden, uncompensated emancipation."[20]

One thing is clear: the proposal was, as Charles Sumner put it, the president's "exclusive & unaided work." Others in the administration tried, to no avail, to dissuade him from his course. Treasury Secretary Salmon Chase, with whom the president shared a draft, urged him not to include a proposal that stood no chance of being adopted; to do so, he cautioned Lincoln, would likely "weaken rather than strengthen yourself and your administration." As Chase foresaw, proposing a plan widely panned as unrealistic further damaged the president's professional reputation in the Washington community—particularly coming as it did on the heels of the disastrous fall elections.[21]

In addition to damaging Lincoln's reputation in the nation's capital, the plan sowed doubts that Lincoln intended to follow through on his promise to deliver the final Emancipation Proclamation on January 1, 1863. Many abolitionists wondered aloud whether Lincoln's message meant he was planning to replace the promised proclamation with a watered-down plan of gradual compensated emancipation. However, this was a misreading of Lincoln's purpose, which Sumner discerned more clearly than most. Sumner conceded that both the president's message and the plan were a "curiosity," but he assured the abolitionist Wendell Phillips that Lincoln's true purpose in the message was "declaring & vindicating Emancipation." Indeed, that Lincoln presented his proposals as constitutional amendments rather than statutes ensured that no action Congress could take would forestall Lincoln issuing the final Emancipation Proclamation come January 1, 1863.[22]

Although Lincoln barely mentioned the Emancipation Proclamation in his December message, he nonetheless tried to use the message to help explain his forthcoming edict. He prefaced the presentation of his three amendments by insisting that slavery was the root cause of the Civil War and of its continuation. "Without slavery the rebellion could never have existed," Lincoln declared, and "without slavery it could not continue." While ostensibly defending the colonization amendment, he avowed that the North had nothing to fear from emancipation, even if not a single freed slave left the country. The moral grandeur so famously lacking in the legalistic proclamation was supplied in the "soaring rhetoric" of the December message's "inspired conclusion." "In giving freedom to the slave," Lincoln announced, "we assure freedom to the free." Fearful of burdening the proclamation with extravagant or extraneous rhetoric that might make it constitutionally vulnerable, Lincoln used his speech to Congress to try to ready the country for a proclamation that would require them to "think anew, and act anew."[23]

CHAPTER 8

"An Act of Justice"
The Final Proclamation

"If the president means to carry out his edict of freedom on the New Year, what is all this stuff about gradual emancipation?"[1] That was a question on the minds of many in the wake of Lincoln's annual message. But while the message may have "sowed doubt" about whether the president still intended to deliver the final proclamation, there appears to have been no doubt in Lincoln's own mind. When a delegation of "unconditional Unionists" from Kentucky came to see him on November 21, he "dwelt upon" the advantages of his plan for gradual abolition but also insisted that "he would rather die than take back a word of the Proclamation." In Lincoln's mind, gradual compensated abolition remained the best policy, the policy applicable to all states, not just those in rebellion, and the policy least subject to constitutional challenge and political reversal once peace came. However, there was no going back on the policy of military emancipation announced in the proclamation.[2]

Perhaps most revealing of Lincoln's state of mind at the close of 1862 was a comment he made to Charles Sumner, who went see the president on the evening of December 27 to deliver a petition urging the president "to stand by the Proclamation." Lincoln told Sumner that "he could not stop the Proclamation if he would, & would not stop it if he could." The meaning of the latter part of this statement is relatively straightforward. He would not stop it if he could because he, like Sumner, judged the proclamation to be militarily necessary and morally just. His decision to issue the final proclamation reflected that conviction.[3]

Less clear is why Lincoln felt that he could not stop the proclamation even if he wanted to. If the proclamation was his decision to make, then why would he feel powerless to prevent it? A clue lies in Lincoln's response to Massachusetts congressman Benjamin Thomas, who at Orville Browning's urging had tried to persuade the president not to issue the proclamation. Lincoln told Thomas that "if he should refuse to issue his proclamation there would be a rebellion in the north, and that a dictator would be placed over his head within a week." The response seems hyperbolic but reflected Lincoln's acute awareness of his precarious political standing in the country, in Washington, and even within his own party.[4]

The war continued to go extremely poorly, and the mood in the reconvened Congress was "sour." Writing on December 10, Congressman Henry Dawes reported to his wife that "this is the darkest day yet, and no ray of light as yet penetrates the thick clouds which hang over us." The following day began the Battle of Fredericksburg, which ended on the 15th with a crushing defeat of the Union army, after which Lincoln's popularity, already sagging, "reached a low ebb." In the immediate wake of Fredericksburg, members of Congress were inundated with criticisms of the administration's "utterly incompetent" handling of the war. A Pennsylvania congressman, for instance, heard from constituents who reported that Lincoln was now "denounced by many of his most devoted friends in former times" and warned that "if things are not more successfully managed, the President will be generally deserted." Writing on the 18th, George Templeton Strong speculated that if things did not turn around soon, the president would be forced to "resign and make way for [Vice President] Hamlin." One of Sumner's correspondents suggested that the president's resignation would not only "be received with great satisfaction" but might "avert what . . . will otherwise come, viz, a violent and bloody revolution at the North."[5]

Republicans could not force Lincoln to resign, although one senator groused that his colleagues would gladly ask for the president's resignation "if they supposed he would take the advice." So instead they set their sights on forcing him to overhaul his cabinet, particularly by ridding it of the man many regarded as Lincoln's "evil genius," Secretary of State William Seward. On December 16 and 17, all thirty-two Republican senators caucused in secret and agreed to dispatch a nine-man delegation to convey their unhappiness with Seward's malign influence and Lincoln's defective leadership and to demand "a change in and partial reconstruction of the Cabinet." Upon learning of the caucus's outcome, Seward immediately submitted his resignation.[6]

Lincoln was stunned. "Rumors swirled through the capital, creating widespread fear that a coup d'etat was underway." Lincoln confessed to Browning on the 18th that since learning of the secret caucus the previous evening, he had been "more distressed than by any event of my life," adding that he felt "sometimes half-disposed to gratify" those who "wish to get rid of me." Echoing Dawes's despairing language, Lincoln told Browning that he could "hardly see a ray of hope." "We are now on the brink of destruction," Lincoln brooded, and it appeared that even "the Almighty is against us."[7]

Lincoln ultimately weathered the cabinet crisis, refusing to accept Seward's resignation and outmaneuvering Secretary of the Treasury Salmon Chase, who had been the senators' "chief informant" and the source of their grossly exaggerated views of Seward's influence over Lincoln. But even while Lincoln managed to defuse "the senatorial putsch," he knew that there was no chance he could defy his party by walking back the proclamation. On December 15, the Republican-dominated Congress had made its views clear by supporting a resolution that backed "the policy of emancipation, as indicated in [Lincoln's] proclamation." The resolution's author was Samuel Fessenden, whose brother, Senator William Fessenden, helped to lead the palace revolution against Seward and who made few efforts to conceal his contempt for Lincoln and his cabinet, which he regarded as the most "shambling . . . set of incapables" ever "collected in our government before, since the world began." In endorsing the proclamation, Republicans in Congress were not so much signaling their support for the president as they were making clear that they would countenance no retreat by the president from his pledge.[8]

Lincoln knew that he had no choice but to "stand firm" and issue the proclamation.[9] Failure to do so would have made him appear weak, even "cowardly," by seeming to take "dictation" from Democrats and slaveholders.[10] Congress, already "a center of anti-Lincoln agitation," would have deserted him. He would have become a president without a party and almost without power, with no prospect of reelection.[11]

The decision facing Lincoln at the end of 1862 was never really about whether to stick with the proclamation or retract it but how to frame it and define its scope. In the days and weeks leading up to the proclamation, the *New York Tribune* reported, Lincoln had been "strongly pressed" by antislavery advocates to place the proclamation "upon high moral ground."[12] Other supporters of the proclamation, though, like John Murray Forbes, counseled that the president eschew the language of "philanthropy or justice" in favor of grounding the proclamation on "the ground of 'military necessity' . . . even more squarely" than he had done in the preliminary proclamation. Forbes warned that many of even the most steadfast Republicans continued to have "constitutional scruples" about emancipation on any other grounds. In addition, only by grounding the proclamation in military exigency could the president hope to attract the support of Democrats and "self-styled 'Conservatives,'" most of whom "do not want to expend their brothers and sons and money for the benefit of the negro, but who will be very glad to see Northern life and treasure saved by any practical measure, even if it does incidentally an act of justice and benevolence." Moreover, the more broadly the measure was "backed up by public opinion," the greater the blow against the rebellion and slavery. Even Forbes, though, wanted "a good strong Proclamation full of vigor, of freedom and of *democracy*."[13]

When Sumner spoke with Lincoln about emancipation on the evening of December 27, he strongly urged that while the proclamation was properly "an act of military necessity & just self-defense, it was also an act of justice and humanity which must have the blessings of a benevolent God." However, when Lincoln convened the cabinet on Monday morning, December 29, to read them the draft of his final proclamation, there was no mention of justice or morality. Instead, Lincoln acted "by virtue of the power in me vested as Commander-in-Chief . . . in time of actual armed rebellion" and cast the proclamation as "a fit and necessary war measure" for suppressing the rebellion. The following evening, after the cabinet had met a second time to discuss the proclamation, the *Tribune*'s correspondent reported that the president was determined to issue the proclamation "as a war measure from the Commander-in-Chief of the Army" and not as a "measure of morality . . . issuing from the bosom of philanthropy." The president's reason, according to the *Tribune*, was to help ensure slaves would be able to "establish judicially their title to freedom" should it be challenged in the courts.¹⁴

Lincoln's insistence on eschewing all mention of morality and justice, however, did not sit well with everybody in the cabinet, particularly Chase, whose views on the matter mirrored Sumner's. On the third of the three consecutive days the cabinet discussed the final proclamation, Chase urged the addition of a final sentence that would put the proclamation upon the "higher ground" that Lincoln had so resolutely resisted. Chase proposed adding: "Upon this act, sincerely believed to be an act of justice warranted by the Constitution, and of duty demanded by the circumstances of the country, I invoke the considerate judgment of Mankind and the gracious favor of Almighty God." Seeing that Chase's "felicitous closing sentence" (in Welles's words) was broadly supported in the cabinet and probably anxious to make some concessions to Chase, who had proposed extensive changes to Lincoln's draft, the president relented and adopted Chase's paragraph, changing only "of duty demanded by the circumstances of the country" to "upon military necessity."¹⁵ In the end, then, Sumner and Chase prevailed in getting Lincoln to justify the proclamation not only as a military necessity but, as Sumner had doggedly insisted, as "an act of justice" that had the "blessings of a benevolent God."¹⁶

Lincoln was also under increasing pressure from supporters to add to the final proclamation a provision relating to the military enlistment of Blacks, something that he had not included in the preliminary proclamation. As Forbes communicated to Sumner on December 27, it was imperative that the president's proclamation be explicit in declaring "not only emancipation but all the fruits thereof in the [government's] perfect right to use the Negro in every respect as a man, and consequently as a soldier, sailor or laborer, wherever he can most effectually strike a blow against the enemy."¹⁷

In July 1862, in an amendment to the Militia Act, Congress had already authorized the president to receive "persons of African descent ... into the service of the United States, for the purpose of constructing intrenchments, or performing camp service, or any other labor, or any military or naval service for which they may be found competent."¹⁸ But while Lincoln was willing to have the army employ Blacks as cooks or laborers on entrenchments, he was reluctant to put guns in their hands. His resistance to using Blacks as combat troops in the Union army may have stemmed in part from Lincoln's lack of confidence in Blacks' fighting capacity, but more important was his fear that it could provoke a backlash among Whites, especially in the border states but also within the military. Lincoln worried—and many close to him echoed the concern—that he could "lose as many whites from the army" as he would gain in Black troops.[19]

However, Lincoln's views about the value of arming slaves evolved rapidly in the latter half of 1862, as had public opinion in the North. By the end of the summer of 1862, Lincoln permitted and sometimes encouraged "local and uncoordinated" efforts to enlist freed slaves, although he avoided "an explicit policy statement for fear of antagonizing Border State sentiment." By the end of the year, though, with no end in sight to the carnage, Lincoln was convinced that the time had come to signal an explicit policy shift and to put the full force of the government behind the enlistment of Black soldiers. In language that at once echoed and stepped beyond the Militia Act, Lincoln closed the draft proclamation with a paragraph that would "declare, and make known" that freed slaves "will be received into the armed services of the United States to garrison forts, positions, stations, and other places, and to man vessels of all sorts in said service."[20]

Not everyone in the cabinet approved. Attorney General Edward Bates considered the paragraph "wholly useless, and probably injurious." In Bates's view, the paragraph was unnecessary because enlistment of Black troops could "be quite as well done without as with the pledge." Even Chase, who strongly supported the enlistment of Black troops, argued that the paragraph was unnecessary in view of the successful efforts to organize Black regiments already under way in places such as Louisiana and South Carolina. He advised Lincoln that it would be best "to omit all reference to the military employment of the enfranchised population, leaving it to the course of things already well begun." Lincoln disagreed, believing there was value in the president formally and publicly authorizing the enlistment of Black soldiers and refused to omit or modify the paragraph.[21]

Although not new, another crucial feature of the final proclamation was the provision stating that the government, including the military, "will recognize and maintain the freedom" of all persons held as slaves in rebel areas. The preliminary proclamation had been more explicit in commanding the government and military not only to "recognize and maintain" slaves' freedom but that come January 1st, federal authorities should "do no act or acts to repress such persons . . . in any efforts they may make for their actual freedom," language that led excitable critics to argue that the administration was attempting to foment "servile insurrection." In his draft of the final proclamation, Lincoln tried to defuse this fear by adding an "appeal to the people so declared to be free, to abstain from all disorder, tumult, and violence, unless in necessary self-defense." The cabinet approved of the language about forswearing violence—although Seward preferred Lincoln to "command and require" the slaves to abstain from violence, a suggestion the president rejected.[22] But even with the disavowal of violence included, Chase and Seward successfully pressed Lincoln to drop the controversial clause in the preliminary proclamation (which was also in his draft of the final proclamation) directing the military not to "repress such persons . . . in any efforts they may make for their actual freedom."[23] However, the change in wording did not alter, even if it may have obscured, the significance of the policy shift. Henceforth, beginning on January 1, 1863, the administration was ushering in what James Oakes calls a "new policy of deliberate enticement."[24]

Slaves had, of course, been fleeing for freedom since the beginning of the Civil War in acts of "self-emancipation."[25] And Congress had already made clear that the army could not be in the business of returning slaves to rebel masters. But while the government's policy prior to the proclamation, as John Hay explained, was "not to return to slavery those slaves who fall necessarily into our hands in the course of the war," it was also "not to entice them in, nor to incite them to rise." The final proclamation renounced incitement but opened the door, even if not explicitly, to a policy of enticement.[26]

A notable departure from the preliminary proclamation was that Lincoln made no mention in the final proclamation of either compensation for slaveowners or colonization for freed slaves, which may have reflected Lincoln's recognition of how poorly his annual message—

particularly its call for colonization—had been received within his own party.[27] Not that Lincoln had given up on either compensation, particularly in the border states, or colonization. Far from it. In fact, on New Year's Eve, the day he and the cabinet were putting the final touches on the proclamation, Lincoln signed a contract with an entrepreneur, Bernard Kock, to transport five thousand freed Blacks to an island off the Haitian coast. While Lincoln may not have quite shared the enthusiasm of Montgomery Blair's sister, who hailed the agreement as "the beginning of the 2nd great Exodus," he was sufficiently eager to see the project succeed that he arranged to have Kock paid $250,000 for the venture, and overrode the strong misgivings of several cabinet members, including Secretary of State Seward and Attorney General Bates, who sized up Kock as an "errant humbug" and "charlatan adventurer." Their skepticism proved well-founded as the venture proved an abject failure, and less than a year after sending nearly 450 Black Americans to the island, Lincoln would be forced to authorize the rescue of the 350 surviving emigrants. The only virtue of the ill-conceived and poorly executed plan was that it seemed, finally, to cure Lincoln of the notion that colonization was a viable way to address the country's racial problems.[28]

Perhaps the most pressing decision facing Lincoln in formulating the final proclamation was which areas to exempt from the edict of emancipation. Indeed, specifying those areas is what made a final proclamation necessary since the preliminary proclamation, following on Congress's instructions in the Second Confiscation Act, pledged that on January 1, 1863, the president would designate "the States, and parts of states, if any" that were "in rebellion against the United States." In the preliminary proclamation, Lincoln stipulated that states would be deemed no longer in rebellion if prior to January 1 they held congressional elections in which a majority of "qualified voters" participated. By electing members to Congress, areas could preserve slavery. The pressing decision Lincoln faced at the end of December was not whether to stick with the proclamation but to determine which areas would be covered by it.[29]

Chase argued strenuously that the final proclamation should not exempt areas within states because such carve outs would invite administrative confusion and "impair, in public estimation, the moral effect of the Proclamation." As a practical matter, Chase pointed out, the exemptions within states would apply only to about a dozen parishes around New Orleans and about a half dozen counties in Virginia, areas that were under Union control and where, consistent with acts of Congress, "the slaves of disloyal masters . . . are already enfranchised; and the slaves of loyal masters are practically so." Indeed, some of the latter had "already commenced paying wages to their laborers." By exempting these areas from the proclamation, Chase feared, Lincoln's order could, in some cases, reestablish slavery. Lincoln, though, insisted on exempting these areas since he had used the preliminary proclamation to induce officials in these areas to hold congressional elections in December.[30]

Lincoln also came under intense pressure from Tennessee Unionists, including Military Governor Andrew Johnson, to exempt the entire state from the proclamation, even though large swaths of it were still under Confederate control and only a quarter of the state's districts had representation in Congress. Johnson tried to hold additional elections in December, but the military situation in those areas made that all but impossible. Following the criteria laid out in the preliminary proclamation, only a few districts, mostly in East Tennessee, a part of the state that had voted against secession in 1861, qualified for exemption from the proclamation. However, eager to "bolster Andrew Johnson's regime and attract cooperation from [the state's] slaveholders," Lincoln acceded to Johnson's pressure campaign and exempted the entire state of Tennessee and its 275,000 slaves from the proclamation.[31]

While exempting Tennessee as well as areas in southern Louisiana and Tidewater, Virginia, Lincoln also chose *not* to exempt many areas in the South that *were* under the control of the Union army, including parts of Arkansas, Florida, Mississippi, North Carolina, and the Sea Islands of South Carolina. As Eric Foner points out, these were generally areas where "the number of white Unionists was small or nonexistent and political reconstruction had made little or no progress," and so Lincoln saw little to be gained politically from exempting them. In these areas, Lincoln's proclamation went into immediate effect on the day he issued it.[32]

Lincoln's flexibility in responding to the "scramble for exemptions" was evident too in his response to the "Forty-eight Counties designated as West-Virginia." Those western counties had refused to join the rest of Virginia in seceding and instead set up a so-called Restored Government of Virginia, with congressional representation. When the forty-eight counties petitioned to be accepted as a new state, Congress assented after the Restored Government agreed to a complex scheme of gradual emancipation in which all children born to slaves in West Virginia after July 4, 1863, would be free, all those under ten would be freed at the age of twenty-one, all those between the ages of ten and twenty-one would be freed at twenty-five, and no slaves could be brought to the state to live there. The bill made it to Lincoln's desk in December 1862 despite strong opposition from those who believed the bill violated the constitutional requirement that a state must consent to its division and from antislavery advocates, including Sumner, who wanted immediate abolition of slavery to be a precondition for statehood.[33]

Lincoln first put the question to his cabinet on December 23 and found it evenly divided, with Stanton, Seward, and Chase in favor of signing the bill and Welles, Bates, and Blair opposing it. The three opponents believed the bill was plainly unconstitutional. The three supporters brushed aside constitutional concerns, arguing that the political advantages of "plant[ing] a free state south of the Ohio" were too great to pass up, although Chase privately told Lincoln that he would have preferred "immediate compensated emancipation" to the gradualist scheme.[34]

On December 31, Lincoln announced that he would sign the bill. West Virginia was too important politically and militarily to "seem to break faith" with her "brave and good men" who justly regarded admission into the Union "as a matter of life and death." In the preliminary proclamation, Lincoln required a state seeking to be exempt from the proclamation to hold elections in which "a majority of the qualified voters of such State shall have participated," but now Lincoln moved the goal posts to get the result he desired. It was not qualified voters who counted "but the qualified voters, *who choose to vote.*" Those who didn't vote didn't matter. After all, Lincoln asked: "Can this government stand if it indulged constitutional constructions by which men in open rebellion against it, are to be accounted, man for man, the equals of those who maintain their loyalty to it?" For Lincoln, the answer was clear, particularly as he was eager to reward the one southern government that had adopted the gradualist model he had championed for so long. Since

West Virginia would not become a state until the following summer, after voters ratified the revised constitution with its provision for the gradual abolition of slavery, Lincoln added West Virginia's forty-eight counties to the list of areas to be exempted from the proclamation.[35]

The day after signing West Virginia's statehood bill, Lincoln affixed his signature to the final Emancipation Proclamation. According to an often-quoted account given years later by Seward's son, who was present at the private signing ceremony in the afternoon, Lincoln declared, immediately before "slowly and carefully" signing his name, that "I never, in my life, felt more certain that I was doing right than I do in signing this paper." In another equally dramatic account—also given many years later—by Lincoln's son, on the morning of January 1st the president's wife Mary Todd Lincoln pressed her husband on what he intended to do, and he looked up, "as to heaven," and replied, "I am a man under orders. I cannot do otherwise."[36]

These dramatic narratives conjure up visions of a resolute president, animated by moral clarity and conviction, issuing a historic decree. The repeated use of the first person keeps our eyes trained squarely on the Great Emancipator and his momentous decision. But Lincoln's certainty that he could not do otherwise than sign the proclamation is evidence less of a president in command than of the constraints on the president's power. By January 1, 1863, there was no alternative left to Lincoln than signing the Emancipation Proclamation. To do otherwise would have been to abdicate party leadership and forfeit presidential power.

Lincoln, of course, made important decisions. He decided about the areas to exempt, decisions based not on moral conviction but calculations of political expediency and the political pressure brought by other politicians. He included language about the enlistment of slaves in the army, but in doing so he was acting in accordance with Congress's clearly expressed wishes and giving formal sanction to the enlistment of Black troops that was already underway. He omitted any mention of colonization and compensation, but not because he had ceased to believe in these policies but because the public reception to these ideas had so often been negative. Few if any presidents have been more gifted or eloquent writers, yet fear that the courts could neuter the proclamation after the war meant Lincoln felt compelled to avoid the stirring moral language that so many sorely wished to see in the document. Only at the very last was he prevailed upon, seemingly against his better judgment, to proclaim it openly as an "act of justice."[37]

In sum, while the proclamation bore the president's signature, it was profoundly shaped by the courts, by acts of Congress, by the input of his cabinet members, by pressure campaigns from politicians and groups, and by public opinion. Even in unilateralism, as political scientist Andrew Rudalevige writes, "there is pluralism."[38]

CHAPTER 9

A Less than Conclusive Order

On New Year's Day 1863, twenty-seven-year-old Moses Coit Tyler, who decades later would become the country's first professor of US history, wrote to his wife with a prediction that "the date at the top of this letter" will become "the *greatest* one for America and perhaps for the human family since July 4, 1776." Only weeks before, Tyler had written to his wife despairingly of battlefield disasters and of "public affairs . . . shrouded with gloom" and marked by "red tape and rottenness," even "imbecility," but Lincoln's Emancipation Proclamation had transformed his mood. For today, he told his wife, "goes forth the glorious edict which strikes off the chains of those millions of slaves and liberates the nation from the viler slavery of a terrible iniquity."[1]

This is the way the Emancipation Proclamation is so often remembered. With the stroke of a pen, the Great Emancipator freed the slaves. The celebrated Italian "Hero of Two Worlds," Giuseppe Garibaldi captured this sentiment in a letter to Lincoln predicting that the proclamation would see him "pass down to posterity under the name of the Emancipator." "An entire race of mankind yoked by selfishness to the collar of Slavery," he gushed, "is *by you* . . . restored to the dignity of Manhood."[2]

This heroic narrative competes with another story line that holds that the proclamation was largely a sham. In this telling, made famous by Richard Hofstadter, the proclamation, which had all "the moral grandeur of a bill of lading," "did not in fact free any slaves," since it emancipated slaves where "its effects could not reach" and kept in bondage those the government could reach.³ Hofstadter's unsparing judgment was hardly original, as such sentiments were commonplace at the time the proclamation was issued. One abolitionist, for instance, expressed his disappointment that the proclamation was "a halfway measure, which purports to give freedom to the bulk of the slave population beyond the reach of our arms, while it ignores or defies justice by clinching the rivets of the chain which binds those whom alone we have present power to redeem." Even those opposed to the proclamation often dismissed it as "practically a dead letter." As one organ of conservative Republicanism opined on January 7, 1863: "The proclamation has been five days before the country in print and the sun, moon, and stars seem to continue in their courses, unmindful of the decree—and the negroes, and white folks too, are pretty much where they were before Abraham Lincoln shed a drop of ink in writing his name at the bottom of a probable sheet of foolscap."⁴

Lincoln's own views on the proclamation were more nuanced. Two months before his assassination, he would tell the painter Francis Carpenter that he considered it "the central act of my administration." And yet he was also acutely aware of its limitations. On the evening before signing the final proclamation, he ushered into his office three abolitionist clergymen who carried with them a petition urging Lincoln to "immediately enact and execute" a "decree of universal freedom" that would liberate every slave in the United States. In the eyes of the petitioners, the president had the power to rid the nation of slavery with a bold stroke of his righteous pen. "Your memorial," a skeptical Lincoln told them, "represents that a decree of emancipation would produce a transfiguration—but I have no evidence that it would." Lincoln derided the notion that there would be something "miraculous in the effect of emancipation." Instead he believed that the proclamation that he was about to sign "would do something" and that it was "on the whole, the best course that could now be pursued."⁵ Having exhausted his other options, it was an "experiment" worth trying. Before ushering them out of his office, Lincoln reminded his guests that "proclaiming slaves free did not make them free," a point he illustrated by drawing from his seemingly boundless reservoir of "homely" anecdotes: "In one of our western courts," Lincoln recounted, "there had been an attempt made to show that a calf had five legs—the way the point was to be established was by calling the tail a leg, but the decision of the judge was that *calling* the tail a leg, did not make it a leg, and the calf had but four legs after all."[6]

Lincoln recognized that words mattered, but he was also keenly aware that a president "does not obtain results . . . merely by giving orders." He instinctively grasped Neustadt's teaching that issuing a command is not the end of politics but the beginning of it. In this sense, Lincoln's "last resort . . . was not 'last' at all." The proclamation was not a final solution so much as a crucial but "less than conclusive order," which signaled an important shift in policy and which "added leverage" and "changed the context" of the persuasive work that lay ahead.[7] Only through political persuasion—and winning the war—could he realize his ultimate goal of ending slavery. It was not the proclamation itself that made Lincoln the Great Emancipator but the subsequent political work that ensured that its words did not end up meaning little more than the "the Pope's bull against the comet."[8]

Lincoln's final proclamation was greeted with celebrations in cities all across the North, but the "culminating event" took place on the night of January 5, 1863, at Cooper Union in New York, the site where Lincoln had given his celebrated antislavery address three years earlier. A packed auditorium, "three-fifths black and two-fifths white," gathered to salute the glorious proclamation. Among the speakers was Henry Highland Garnet, a prominent Black preacher and radical abolitionist who had escaped from slavery as a child. Garnet praised Lincoln for keeping his "eyes set on the God of Justice" in signing the much-anticipated proclamation, and thundered that "no power could ever undo what [the president] had done." The reality, however, as Lincoln was well aware, was there were many earthly powers that could undo or blunt the proclamation, including the Confederate army, the Democratic Party, the courts, state governments, and public opinion. The president could command none of these other actors, even in wartime. Indeed, even commanding his own military to follow the proclamation was not as straightforward as it might seem at first.[9]

The proclamation purported to transform Union armies into "de facto armies of liberation," but it could not so readily convert soldiers into supporters of emancipation. That Union soldiers voted overwhelmingly for Lincoln in 1864 has tended to obscure the intense opposition to the proclamation felt by many enlisted men and officers, particularly those who were Democrats and from border states. As historian Jonathan White has shown, the proclamation "pushed many Democrats out of the service in the winter and spring of 1863" because they refused to fight for the freedom of a people they despised. At the end of January 1863, one Wisconsin soldier reported that many soldiers from border states were "deserting & going home every day" because they "say they didn't come down here to free the niggers." Trials for desertion spiked between January and March 1863, while morale in the Union armies reached "an all-time low" during these months. Egged on by Democratic politicians and newspapers, many soldiers refused to reenlist when their term of service was finished and many officers resigned—or tried to—rather than fight in a war for Black liberation.[10]

The responsibility for explaining and promoting compliance with the new policy of enticement and the recruitment of Black troops in the western theater was assigned to Adjutant General Lorenzo Thomas. Sent to the Mississippi Valley at the end of March 1863, Thomas gave speeches to Union troops throughout the spring explaining why the administration had "determined to take from the rebels . . . their Negroes, and [thereby] compel them to send back a portion of their whites to cultivate their deserted plantations" or else "their armies will starve." Persuasion, though, was coupled with the threat of coercion. Thomas warned sternly that "no opposition on the part of officers and soldiers will be allowed." After one regiment greeted Thomas's expounding of the new policy with hissing, he had the regiment's officers arrested.[11]

Some historians have argued that slaves "taught" Union soldiers the "lesson" of emancipation by fleeing slavery for the freedom to be gained behind army lines. But this account slights the many ways, as White shows, that the "Lincoln administration, the Republican majority in Congress, and the commanding officers in the field" attempted to instill in Union soldiers—"sometimes by force, sometimes by intimidation, sometimes by persuasion, and sometimes through the deprivation of opposing viewpoints"—a belief in the legitimacy of emancipation as a war aim. To combat antiwar propaganda and "growing discontent," officers banned Democratic newspapers from Union camps and "arrested, court-martialed, and punished" those who criticized Lincoln or the policy of emancipation.[12]

Another common mechanism for manufacturing consent in the early spring of 1863 was the adoption of regimental resolutions that praised Lincoln's proclamation and condemned the treason of the Copperheads. The language of these many resolutions was sufficiently similar to suggest that they were, in many cases, "ordered from the top down." Drafted by Union officers, approved by enlisted soldiers under threat of ostracism or punishment, and published in local newspapers, these public displays of support for emancipation were "part of a mechanism for raising morale, discouraging desertion, and attempting to transform the ideological beliefs of the soldiery."[13]

No amount of teaching or intimidation or even coercion, however, could ensure full compliance with the proclamation in every theater of the war. Throughout the Civil War, James Oakes observes, "Union authorities ... were bedeviled by reports of individual Union soldiers, particularly from the Border States, who resisted federal emancipation policy and abused their contrabands." In the war's final, harsh winter, for instance, a Kentucky-born general in charge of Camp Nelson, the state's largest recruiting center for African American soldiers, expelled all the family members of Black soldiers from the camp. The general's order was overturned a week later, but not before one hundred Black women and children perished from cold and hunger.[14]

Even where military officers were fully in sympathy with Lincoln's proclamation, implementation was far from automatic or immediate. Ulysses Grant embraced the president's proclamation wholeheartedly, promptly instructing "all commanders" to "exert themselves in carrying out the policy of the Administration, not only in organizing colored regiments, and rendering them efficient, but also in removing prejudice against them." Yet in the middle of February 1863, concerned about maintaining secrecy about what the army was doing, Grant "positively forbid" his troops from "enticing ... negroes to leave their homes to come within the lines of the army." Indeed, he instructed the army that "no [unauthorized] persons, white or black" should be allowed into camp. Instead Blacks should "remain at their homes" and, where possible, be allowed, in the words of the proclamation, to "labor faithfully for reasonable wages."[15]

Grant's directive not to entice or even accept runaway slaves brought a rebuke six weeks later from General in Chief Henry Halleck, who explained to Grant that the "policy of this Government" is "to withdraw from the enemy as much productive labor as possible," which meant withdrawing "from the use of the enemy all the slaves you can." It was therefore imperative that no one in the Union army ever "discourage the Negroes from coming under our protection." Grant's directive was "not only bad policy in itself... but is directly opposed to the policy adopted by the Government." In April, two months after his original order, Grant reversed himself, instructing his subordinates to "encourage all negroes, particularly middle-aged males, to come within our lines."[16]

Little wonder, then, that it was not until around June of 1863, as Oakes reports, that "evidence of truly large numbers of slaves 'collected' or 'captured' by Union troops begins to appear in official reports as well as in letters and diaries of individual soldiers." Only six months after the proclamation was issued did the Union army truly become "an army of liberation in the seceded states."[17]

Within the military, the administration could and did rely on coercion and command where persuasion was insufficient to ensure compliance. But in dealing with other institutions of government as well as public opinion, persuasion was essential to ensuring that the Emancipation Proclamation would fulfill its promise that slaves "henceforward shall be free," as Lincoln fully recognized.[18]

The need to publicly defend the proclamation, ironically, had become even more acute as the military outlook brightened in the summer of 1863. The Siege of Vicksburg gave the Union army complete control of the Mississippi River, and, almost simultaneously, the climactic Battle of Gettysburg dealt a crushing blow to Lee's army. The Union's stunning success in early July, however, raised the "disturbing possibility for Lincoln and the Republicans [that] the war might end without slavery having been destroyed." With the overwhelming majority of slaves in the Confederacy still enslaved, Democrats seized on the Union victories in Gettysburg and Vicksburg to intensify calls for the administration to open peace negotiations with a weakened Confederacy that would put an end to the fighting, restore "the Union as it was," and abandon the Emancipation Proclamation.[19]

The "no-nonsense" proclamation had "explained very little" about its purpose or rationale, but in August Lincoln seized upon an invitation to speak to a mass meeting of "unconditional Union-men" in Springfield to pen a lengthy public letter defending the proclamation. Lincoln asked that the letter be read aloud at the meeting—and "very slowly" to ensure all heard it—but the audience he most wished to address was not his "old political friends" in attendance but all those Americans who were "dissatisfied" with him for seemingly transforming a war to preserve the Union into a war for Black freedom.[20]

He began by acknowledging the powerful desire for peace but emphasized that the only way to achieve peace short of relinquishing the Union was for the army to finish the job and crush the rebellion. Talk of a "peace compromise" was a distraction that would only "waste time" and enable the enemy to regroup and "improve to our disadvantage." Lincoln then came directly to the point: "To be plain, you are dissatisfied with me about the negro." He acknowledged that "quite likely" there was "a difference of opinion" between them on that subject: "I certainly wish that all men could be free, while I suppose you do not." Having claimed freedom's high ground, Lincoln averred that this difference of opinion should not matter in weighing the wisdom and legitimacy of the proclamation because, like every action he had taken as commander in chief, it was done with the sole purpose of suppressing the rebellion by force of arms, which was the only practical way of restoring the Union.[21]

Lincoln squarely met the objections of those who "dislike the emancipation proclamation, and perhaps, would have it retracted." He defended the legal right of the nation and its commander in chief to follow "the law of war in time of war." If slaves were property, as the South claimed, then there was no question that the Union army was justified in seizing the property when needed. After all, "Armies, the world over, destroy enemies' property when they cannot use it; and even destroy their own to keep it from the enemy. Civilized belligerents do all in their power to help themselves, or hurt the enemy, except a few things regarded as barbarous or cruel."[22]

To bolster his claims about the need for the proclamation, Lincoln appealed to the authority of his own military commanders, who "believe the emancipation policy and the use of the colored troops constitute the heaviest blow yet dealt to the rebellion." Indeed, they had told him that at least one of "these important successes could not have been achieved when it was but for the aid of black soldiers." Among the commanders who expressed these views, Lincoln emphasized, were some who "never had any affinity with what is called Abolitionism, or with Republican party politics." Their views were offered "purely as military opinions."[23]

In Lincoln's telling, the case for military necessity seemed self-evident: "I thought that in your struggle for the Union, to whatever extent the negroes should cease helping the enemy, to that extent it weakened the enemy in his resistance to you. Do you think differently? I thought that whatever negroes can be got to do as soldiers, leaves just so much less for white soldiers to do in saving the Union. Does it appear otherwise to you?" How could it not help the Union's cause and undermine the Confederacy to deprive the South of its labor force and augment the fighting power of the Union armies? To ask the question was to answer it.[24]

Lincoln then turned the screw: "You say you will not fight to free negroes. Some of them seem willing to fight for you; but no matter. Fight you, then, exclusively to save the Union." Indeed, he had issued the proclamation for that express purpose: "to aid you in saving the Union." Only after "all resistance to the Union" had been defeated, "if I shall urge you to continue fighting," then and only then "will be an apt time ... to declare you will not fight to free negroes." But Lincoln also made it clear that he would neither revoke the proclamation nor abandon those who had fought for their freedom. He explained that "negroes, like other people, act upon motives. Why should they do anything for us if we will do nothing for them? If they stake their lives for us they must be prompted by the strongest motive, even the promise of freedom. And the promise, being made, must be kept." The proclamation was both a military necessity and a solemn pact.[25]

A confident Lincoln ended on a hopeful note about the war: "Peace does not appear so distant as it did." However, when peace came, Lincoln stressed, it must *"come as to be worth the keeping in all future time."* It must vindicate the principle that "among free men there can be no successful appeal from the ballot to the bullet, and that they who take such appeal are sure to lose their case and pay the cost." The implication was clear: the cost the South must pay and the future worth keeping were the same—a nation without slavery. When victory came, Lincoln closed, "then there will be some black men who can remember that with silent tongue, and clenched teeth, and steady eye, and well-poised bayonet, they have helped mankind on to this great consummation, while I fear there will be some white ones unable to forget that with malignant heart and deceitful speech they strove to hinder it." Lincoln left no doubt that those who backed the Emancipation Proclamation would find themselves on the right side of history.[26]

An address that began by speaking directly to the proclamation's critics—which he addressed as "you" no fewer than thirty-eight times—culminated in the final paragraphs in a resounding rallying cry for the proclamation's supporters. The largely sympathetic Springfield crowd, estimated between fifty-thousand and seventy-five thousand strong, reserved their most vehement cheers for Lincoln's vow to keep his promise of freedom. Antislavery Republicans across the country hailed the president's "true and noble letter" for making clear that the proclamation was not merely a "temporary expedient" that could be sacrificed as part of a negotiated peace but an unbreakable guarantee of freedom.[27]

While Lincoln's vigorous if "frankly partisan" defense of the proclamation was met with widespread acclaim from Republican supporters, many of whom viewed it as "the keynote of the next presidential campaign," it also underscored the proclamation's continuing political vulnerability. Lincoln may have hoped to persuade conservative Unionists of its necessity if not its justice, but he was largely powerless to alter the fact that the proclamation remained highly politicized along partisan lines, with Democrats almost universally opposed and Republicans increasingly supportive. As a result, its fate was inextricably tied up with electoral politics.[28]

If victories on the battlefield raised the prospect of a premature peace upending the proclamation and leaving slavery in place throughout most of the South, military defeats brought the danger of a discontented populace taking it out on an unpopular president and his party at the ballot box, as happened in the fall elections in 1862. Lincoln's refusal to retreat from his pledge of emancipation would mean little if the Democrats won back the presidency in 1864—an office they had controlled for most of the three decades before the war.

Public optimism about the war's recent successes—and the Republicans' success in casting the opposition party as disloyal—helped to buoy the Republican Party in the 1863 fall elections, enabling them to triumph in local elections and gubernatorial contests across the North, including in high stakes contests in Ohio and Pennsylvania. In the aftermath of the fall's electoral victories and the acclaim for his Springfield letter, Lincoln was hailed as "the most popular man in the United States." The following June he was resoundingly renominated by his party.[29]

By the end of the summer of 1864, however, with the Union army's military offensive seemingly stalled, the political momentum shifted dramatically. With no end to the war in sight and the public "getting tired of the war," Lincoln's public support cratered. In August, Lincoln predicted that "unless some great change takes place" he would be "badly beaten" in November, a judgment widely shared within the party.[30] Panicked Republicans mounted a desperate effort to dump Lincoln from the ticket. The Republican Party national chairman Henry Raymond, who Lincoln called "my lieutenant general in politics," informed the president on August 22nd that he had communicated with the administration's "staunchest friends in every State," and "from them all I hear but one report. The tide is setting strongly against us." The two most important causes "assigned for this great reaction in public sentiment," Raymond reported, was "the want of military success" and the belief "that we are not to have peace *in any event* under this Administration until Slavery is abandoned." As the war ground on, the "fear and suspicion" that White Americans were continuing to die only for the sake of ensuring the freedom of Black Americans seemed to be threatening to sink the president's reelection chances and the party's fortunes—and with it the Emancipation Proclamation.[31]

Shortly after receiving Raymond's gloomy assessment of his reelection prospects, Lincoln summoned Frederick Douglass to the White House, who found the president in a state of great agitation. Believing it "exceedingly probable" that he would be defeated in November, Lincoln sought Douglass's help in maximizing the proclamation's impact in the remaining months of his term. The trouble, Lincoln explained, was that "slaves are not coming so rapidly and so numerously to us as I had hoped." Douglass pointed out that part of the problem was that slaveholders made every effort to keep information from slaves and "probably very few knew of his proclamation." Another obstacle thwarting the proclamation's effect was that wealthy slaveowners were able to "refugee" their slaves by transporting them "away from enemy lines and out of the way of an advancing Union army."[32]

The Lincoln administration had already invested considerable resources to help news of the proclamation reach slaves. The War Department had dispatched more than two hundred agents "to go onto southern farms and plantations, where they announced to slaves that they had been freed by proclamation." But all of these recruiters were White. Lincoln asked Douglass to recruit Black agents who he hoped might be more successful in persuading slaves of "the necessity of making their escape." The task Lincoln had in mind was not merely a matter of informing slaves of the existence of the proclamation—the so-called grapevine telegraph often performed this function tolerably well—but of disabusing slaves of the idea that the proclamation would somehow automatically set them free at the war's end. Instead, they had to understand that "should peace be concluded while they remain within the Rebel lines" there was a strong likelihood that they would remain slaves. The Emancipation Proclamation, Lincoln underscored, could not be counted on to abolish slavery.[33]

Taken aback by Lincoln's sense of urgency and "the realization that abolition was anything but certain," Douglass returned home and swiftly drew up a plan for a team of Black agents, "whose business should be somewhat after the original plan of John Brown, to go into the rebel States, beyond the lines of our armies, and carry the news of emancipation, and urge the slaves to come within our boundaries." In the end, the plan never got off the ground, thanks to a reversal in the Union army's fortunes and the subsequent rebound in the Republicans' electoral prospects. The meeting, however, did forever change Douglass's judgment of Lincoln. Just a few weeks before the meeting, Douglass had privately described Lincoln as a man who did "evil by choice, right from necessity," yet now Douglass felt compelled to acknowledge that the president "showed a deeper moral conviction against slavery" than he had credited him with before. Douglass believed Lincoln when he declared, "I hate slavery as much as you do, and I want to see it abolished altogether."[34]

For Lincoln, his meeting with Douglass represented a dramatic shift from the cautionary approach he had generally taken before in meetings with abolitionists who invariably urged the president to be bolder. A month after issuing the final proclamation, for instance, Lincoln met with several prominent abolitionists, including Wendell Phillips and Moncure Conway, who pressed Lincoln about the proclamation's implementation. Among their complaints was that Lincoln's generals were not sufficiently committed to "carry[ing] out the proclamation in good faith by freeing . . . as many as possible of those declared free." Lincoln countered by highlighting the many difficulties the army faced in accommodating runaway slaves. According to Conway, Lincoln told the group that if "I should put in the South these anti-slavery generals and governors, what could they do with the slaves that would come to them?"[35]

Lincoln's response dismayed Conway, who saw it as further evidence that the president lacked the will to end slavery. But Lincoln's answer highlighted a real problem that hampered the proclamation from the outset—namely, that the army "was never prepared" to care for the large number of slaves who came within its lines. From the earliest days of the war, Lincoln and Stanton were peppered with communiques from commanding officers asking how they were supposed to cope, and as the number of slaves entering Union lines climbed higher after the proclamation, so too did the army's struggles in feeding and providing shelter for them, many of whom arrived "half-starved after strenuous escapes or having borne the brunt of wartime shortages on their own farms and plantations." In an effort to manage the growing problem, the government set up "contraband camps," but as their numbers swelled, the "camps soon became notorious for their filth [and] disease," with "outbreaks of dysentery" not uncommon. Lincoln's cautionary note to Conway reflected not a lack of antislavery conviction, as Conway assumed, but his awareness of the practical and ethical difficulties that limited the government's ability to effectively implement the enticement strategy that the proclamation promised.[36]

Although Lincoln's conversations with Douglass and Conway might seem contradictory, both underscored what Oakes calls "the great paradox of military emancipation"—namely, that "although the Union army was overwhelmed by the numbers of contrabands entering its lines, those numbers were never more than a small fraction of the slaves in the rebel states." At the time Douglass spoke with Lincoln in August 1864 the percentage of slaves in the Confederacy that had been freed by the Union army was only about 10 percent. Indeed, at the time of Lee's surrender in April 1865, around 86 percent of the more than 3.5 million slaves in the Confederacy remained enslaved.[37]

The proclamation was an inherently less than conclusive order because American slavery was a vast empire, "by far the largest slave society in the world, possibly the largest in the history of the world." It was numerically huge and territorially vast, and even the Union army, with seven hundred thousand soldiers at its peak, lacked "enough men to physically reach and emancipate more than a fraction of the slaves." As Oakes points out, General William Tecumseh Sherman's devastating March to the Sea, from Atlanta to Savannah at the end of 1864, "cut a ten-mile path of destruction wherever they went, but their marches traced a thin ribbon over Georgia's vast terrain and so swept up only a fraction of the state's slaves." Ten thousand freed slaves marched with Sherman's army, but that was only a sliver of Georgia's slave population, which numbered half a million.[38]

The policy of military emancipation announced in the Emancipation Proclamation and authorized by Congress helped to free several hundred thousand slaves and played a key role in turning the tide in the Civil War, both by disrupting the southern economy and, especially, by enlisting in the Union army as many as one hundred and eighty thousand Black men, who made up nearly one-fifth of the Union's military force by the end of the war.[39] But however indispensable Black troops were to the Union war effort, the shortcomings of military emancipation as a method of eradicating slavery were clear.[40]

Lincoln understood early on that the proclamation's effectiveness in ending slavery depended on Union victories on the battlefield and Republican victories at the ballot box. But what he and other Republicans increasingly came to realize was that Union victories and even Lincoln's reelection were no guarantee that slavery would be destroyed. No matter how extravagantly the Emancipation Proclamation might be praised, it could not itself do the crucial political work of uprooting slavery from American soil. No presidential edict could achieve that. Instead, the destruction of slavery would require the passage of a thirteenth amendment to the US Constitution.

CONCLUSION: LESSONS AND LEGACIES

Few presidential edicts are more famous or misunderstood than the Emancipation Proclamation. The most culturally resonant myth about the proclamation is that President Lincoln freed the slaves with a bold stroke of his pen. That mythology deifies Lincoln as the sagacious Great Emancipator and constructs a narrative of American history centered around the heroic deeds of our "great" presidents. In this narrative, the Emancipation Proclamation sits at the pinnacle of presidential achievement, the noblest deed of our preeminent president.

In our more cynical time, that heroic mythology competes with a more jaded view that the proclamation was much ado about nothing, a largely hollow gesture that freed no slaves at all and lacked even a moral indictment of slavery. On this telling, Lincoln was at best a pusillanimous politician, "a follower and not a leader of public opinion," as Richard Hofstadter put it, or, at worst, a racist at heart who thwarted emancipation at every turn before being "forced into glory," as Leonard Bennett suggested.[1] If there are heroes in this emancipation story, that heroism is to be found in the many thousands of slaves who risked their lives to emancipate themselves by fleeing for the protection of the Union army and in that righteous minority of abolitionists, White and Black, who relentlessly pressed the powers that be, including a reluctant president, to take action.

As radically different as these interpretations are, they share an important assumption about presidential power. Both, in Eugène Pelletan's words, "reason as though Mr. Lincoln wielded a dictatorial unrestricted power, accounting solely to the God of his conscience."[2] Both see in the presidency, in the hands of the right president, an institution of unbounded strength and transformative powers. The one sees in Lincoln's Emancipation Proclamation the realization and validation of the presidency's immense unilateral powers; the other sees in it an inexcusable failure to harness those vast powers of command to lead the fight for social justice. The triumphalism and the disappointment are both reflections of a shared faith in the promise and power of the unilateral presidency.

I have suggested that we instead view President Lincoln and the Emancipation Proclamation through the lens of presidential weakness. As Richard Neustadt teaches us, "even a 'strong' President is weak."[3] Beginning from that premise, we can better understand and even appreciate Lincoln's presidential leadership and his most famous proclamation.

Presidential weakness suffuses the history of the Emancipation Proclamation. The last thing Lincoln initially wanted was a unilateral proclamation of emancipation. Instead he wanted to persuade the border states to endorse his plan for gradual, compensated abolition, preferably coupled with some level of voluntary colonization. That route, Lincoln believed, would be better for the nation because it could shorten the war, minimize social disruption, and create broader acceptance of social change, thereby lessening White backlash. It would also be less vulnerable to the legal challenges that he thought unilateral emancipation would inevitably invite, particularly once the fighting was finished. Only after being rebuffed time and time again by the border states in his efforts to achieve what John Hay called "the object nearest the President's heart" did Lincoln finally, and with great reluctance, turn to playing what he regarded as his final card.[4] The Emancipation Proclamation was Lincoln's last resort.

When Lincoln finally did make up his mind to play that last card in the summer of 1862, he found that he lacked the political support within his own executive branch to do so. Persuaded by advisers to delay announcing the proclamation until he was in a stronger political position, he finally issued the preliminary order at the end of September, the day before the sixty-day clock that Congress had mandated in the Second Confiscation Act was about to expire. That act, which Lincoln had signed only with the greatest reluctance, stipulated that rebels must relinquish their arms by September 24 or face confiscation of all their property, including their slaves. As James Oakes notes, Congress, not the president (or at least not the president acting alone), "made universal emancipation in the rebellious states the de facto policy of the federal government."[5] In issuing the preliminary proclamation, Lincoln was complying with the will of Congress, not asserting his own policy.

Similarly, in the final proclamation, in which Lincoln approved the enlistment of Black troops, he was following the path marked out by Congress, specifically in the Militia Act, passed in July 1862, which allowed the president to enlist "persons of African descent" in "any military or naval service for which they may be found competent." That same act also removed "free" and "white" from the qualifications for military service, which cleared the way for Lincoln's order. In authorizing Black enlistment, Lincoln also depended on the collaboration of Attorney General Edward Bates, whose legal opinion at the end of November 1862 found, contrary to the Supreme Court's ruling in the *Dred Scott* case, that slaves born in the United States were citizens. Even had Lincoln wished to enlist Black troops earlier in the war, he could not have done so.[6]

The delay in issuing the proclamation also highlights the ways in which public opinion constrains the unilateral executive. As Dino Christenson and Douglas Kriner find in their study of unilateral directives, "the causal arrows run from approval to executive action, but not vice versa."[7] In deciding to issue the proclamation, as well as in the framing and content of the proclamation, Lincoln paid close heed to what he thought public opinion would support and how he thought other political elites would receive the order. Lincoln never believed those who assured him that issuing the proclamation would suddenly transform public attitudes about slavery and rally a weary nation behind his lead.

Lincoln's political weakness is perhaps nowhere more obvious than in what he left out of the Emancipation Proclamation. Fearing that the proclamation would be vulnerable to legal challenge at the federal and state level, and perhaps in the court of public opinion too, he resolutely resisted efforts to get him to place the Emancipation Proclamation on "high moral ground." He snuck a few soaring if somewhat mystifying paragraphs into his annual message, and at the last relented to call the proclamation "an act of justice," but that was as far as "the eloquent president" felt able to go.[8] Nothing screams presidential weakness more loudly than Lincoln's need to forswear the "moral grandeur" that generations of critics have never tired of lamenting.

The weakness of the presidency is also lying in plain sight in the famously limited scope of the proclamation. The common complaint that the proclamation freed no slaves because it applied only to those areas where "its effect could not reach" reveals how constrained Lincoln's power of command was by his need for the support of other political actors. Unilaterally emancipating slaves in the border states was never a viable option since nobody apart from a small cadre of activists thought the president possessed that power. More importantly, Lincoln knew that such an audacious act would have pushed those states into the arms of the Confederacy, thereby losing the war, breaking up the Union, and preserving slavery. Lincoln could have unilaterally refused to exempt Tennessee, West Virginia, and a handful of counties in Louisiana and Virginia from the proclamation, but he opted for bargaining rather than command because he thought, probably correctly, that the war effort would be more successful and the proclamation therefore more effective by securing the political support of the political leaders in these key areas.

Lincoln understood what the proclamation's detractors have too often elided—namely, that the proclamation exerted substantial pressure on the exempted areas to free slaves while still enabling those who favored emancipation to triumph in the state elections that were key to abolishing slavery. Even one of Lincoln's most exacting critics, Wendell Phillips, recognized at the time that the exemptions were of little importance: "What care the counties of Louisiana whether they are excepted by the Proclamation or not? With every surrounding locality free, how can they keep their slaves?" The border states, Phillips predicted, would feel the same pressure and soon follow down the path of emancipation.[9] And in fact, by the war's end, as Oakes points out, all the exempted states except Delaware and Kentucky had abolished slavery, while only one state (Arkansas) not exempted by the proclamation had done so.[10] In Maryland, pro-emancipation forces were able to win a majority of state legislative seats in November 1863, which in turn enabled them to call a constitutional convention that elected a majority of pro-emancipation delegates in the spring of 1864, followed by a popular vote in favor of immediate abolition in October 1864, a contest decided by a mere 375 votes out of sixty thousand votes cast.[11] Lincoln's emancipation edict, in short, was not an empty gesture but an important step that, in Neustadt's language, "changed the context" and gave Lincoln "added leverage" in his effort to persuade the border states to abolish slavery.[12]

The proclamation also did vital work, as we saw in chapter 8, in accelerating the recruitment of Black troops and shifting the administration policy toward the active enticement of slaves to flee their masters. Both policy changes strengthened the Union war effort and weakened the Confederacy. Making emancipation an explicit aim of the war also helped to scotch Jefferson Davis's efforts to persuade England and France to recognize the Confederacy as a sovereign nation. Moreover, contrary to the canard that the proclamation freed no slaves, as many as fifty thousand slaves were freed in areas of the South that were under Union control on January 1, 1863, but were not exempt from the proclamation.[13] Perhaps, too, as some scholars have suggested, the proclamation deserves credit for preparing the ground for the Thirteenth Amendment by fostering "the expectation among northerners that when the war was over, slavery would be fully destroyed." In this sense, Oakes writes, the proclamation "helped forge the political will to do what emancipation itself could not do—abolish slavery everywhere in the United States."[14]

If the skeptical reading of the proclamation is guilty at times of obscuring or giving too little weight to the proclamation's importance, it correctly highlights that the proclamation did not guarantee the end of slavery.[15] Like most unilateral executive actions, it was "a less than conclusive order." There was no irrevocable logic that led from the Emancipation Proclamation to the end of slavery. Without Republican victories in the presidential and congressional elections of 1864 and without the Union's defeat of the rebels, slavery would have remained entrenched throughout the South and many of those freed by the edict of the proclamation likely would have been enslaved again. The president's proclamation was neither the beginning nor the culmination of the wartime effort to end slavery.[16]

The skeptical reading is useful in insisting that we look beyond the "singular act of a single man" to the many congressional statutes, state actions, and advocacy groups that contributed to the destruction of slavery in the United States. Such a reading not only helpfully highlights the groups that pushed and sometimes forced—as well as enabled—Lincoln to act, but also invites us to take a more critical lens to the heroic narrative of Lincoln as "the master politician" possessed of an unerring sense of timing who, almost from the outset of the Civil War, maneuvered skillfully to make it a war of emancipation.[17]

In the case of the Emancipation Proclamation, Lincoln was not playing four-dimensional chess. Nor was he running rings around the spinning heads of lesser politicians. During the first two years of the war, as Eric Foner points out, Lincoln "succumbed to wishful thinking about the extent of southern Unionism, the willingness of border slaveholders to accept any plan of emancipation, and the receptivity of black Americans to the fantastic scheme of colonization." The timing of the proclamation, moreover, was far from shrewd. By issuing the proclamation suspending the writ of habeas corpus only two days after announcing the Emancipation Proclamation, as Mark Neely has emphasized, Lincoln "allowed his critics to label his act of liberation a part of a pattern of despotic rule."[18] And by issuing both proclamations only weeks before the start of crucial fall elections, Lincoln handicapped his party in key state and congressional races. Between the summer of 1862 and January 1, 1863, Lincoln's public statements about emancipation arguably did more to confuse the public, demoralize his supporters, and harden opposition than they did to prepare the ground or rally support for the Emancipation Proclamation. Certainly, Lincoln consistently failed to persuade others to support his preferred policy of gradual emancipation paired with compensation for slaveowners. Lincoln's failures and missteps, in sum, were at least as notable as his successes.

Lincoln's great virtue, however, one not generally appreciated by his most exacting critics, was his keen appreciation of the limits of unilateral action. He was decidedly more sophisticated than the legions of impatient advocates who insisted that he could instantly abolish slavery with the stroke of his pen. Unlike Charles Sumner, he never assumed his powers were "God-like."[19] He knew that the president's power is limited. And unlike Horace Greeley, he never entertained the fantasy that declaring every slave in the Confederacy free on the day he was inaugurated would have made those slaves free.[20] He understood that the efficacy of a proclamation depended on far more than his own volition. Although forced to rely on command, Lincoln was never under any illusion that command could substitute for persuasion. As much as Lincoln suffered from wishful thinking throughout 1862, overestimating his persuasive powers and underestimating the tenacity with which border states would cling to slavery and Blacks would resist colonization, he understood that he needed to build support for his emancipation edict for it to be successful. It did no good to command if others would not follow.

Lincoln's understanding of the limits of command helps to explain why the Emancipation Proclamation was a last resort. Lincoln was loath to rely on a unilateral directive not only because he was convinced that his plan of congressionally authorized gradual compensated emancipation was ultimately better for the country but because he recognized that a proclamation of emancipation was not the trump card that some believed. Perhaps better than anyone, Lincoln understood that simply declaring slaves free would not make them free let alone equal citizens.

By deifying Lincoln and canonizing the Emancipation Proclamation, the mythology of Lincoln the Emancipator does a civic disservice by training citizens to look to the president and his unilateral powers for easy solutions, cast in bold, dramatic strokes. In effacing the complexities of history and politics, the myth nurtures a presidency-centric view of our politics that stokes unreasonable expectations about what can be achieved through unilateral action, thereby inviting a corrosive cycle of disillusion as contemporary presidents fail to measure up to the myth of unilateral deliverance. Ironically, this mythology obscures what Lincoln knew so well: that unilateral action is no substitute for the laborious work of politics, of winning elections, mobilizing supporters, cajoling doubters, and bargaining with peers—that presidential power, in short, is the power to persuade.

NOTES

INTRODUCTION: LINCOLN AS LEADER, NEUSTADT AS TEACHER

1. Richard E. Neustadt, *Presidential Power: The Politics of Leadership* (New York: Wiley, 1960), 10; unless otherwise indicated, all subsequent references to *Presidential Power* are to the 1960 edition.
2. Neustadt, *Presidential Power*, 2–3.
3. Neustadt, 2–3, 5, x.
4. Neustadt, x. The quote in the final sentence is from the preface to the 1980 edition of *Presidential Power* (xi) and was repeated in the preface to the 1990 edition (ix). Moreover, much of what Neustadt saw as distinctive about the modern "mid-century" presidency, such as the weakening of party ties and ticket splitting, turned out to be transitory characteristics (4), arguably giving the twenty-first century presidency more in common with the presidency of the nineteenth century than the mid-twentieth century.
5. Neustadt, 24, 27.
6. Neustadt, 27–29.
7. Neustadt, ix.
8. George C. Edwards III, *On Deaf Ears: The Limits of the Bully Pulpit* (New Haven, CT: Yale University Press, 2003). Also see George C. Edwards III, *The Strategic President: Persuasion and Opportunity in Presidential Leadership* (Princeton, NJ: Princeton University Press, 2009); *Predicting the Presidency: The Potential of Persuasive Leadership* (Princeton, NJ: Princeton University Press, 2016); and *Changing Their Minds? Donald Trump and Presidential Leadership* (Chicago: University of Chicago Press, 2021).
9. Neustadt, *Presidential Power*, 29–30.
10. Neustadt, 30–32.
11. Dino P. Christenson and Douglas L. Kriner, *The Myth of the Imperial Presidency: How Public Opinion Checks the Unilateral Executive* (Chicago: University of Chicago Press, 2020), 7, 22. Christenson and Kriner show that most of Bush and Obama's major unilateral directives were popular, although they find Trump was a notable exception to this pattern (148–170).
12. Allen C. Guelzo, *Lincoln's Emancipation Proclamation: The End of Slavery in America* (New York: Simon & Schuster, 2004), 171. Also see Frances Carpenter, *The Inner Life of Abraham Lincoln: Six Months at the White House* (Lincoln: University of Nebraska Press, 1985), 21.
13. Louis Masur, *Lincoln's Hundred Days: The Emancipation Proclamation and the War for the Union* (Cambridge, MA: Harvard University Press, 2012), 186, 184; Guelzo, *Lincoln's Emancipation Proclamation*, 279; Christenson and Kriner, *The Myth of the Imperial Presidency*.

CHAPTER 1. A COMMAND ABORTED

1. Louis Masur, *Lincoln's Hundred Days: The Emancipation Proclamation and the War for the Union* (Cambridge, MA: Harvard University Press, 2012), 24, the "thunder clap" quotation is from the *Chicago Tribune*, September 5, 1861; Allan Nevins, *Frémont: Pathmarker of the West* (New York: Frederick Ungar, 1961), 501, 504; James M. McPherson, *The Struggle for Equality: Abolitionists and the Negro in the Civil War and Reconstruction* (Princeton, NJ: Princeton University Press, 1964), 72–73.

2. Michael Burlingame, ed., *With Lincoln in the White House: Letters, Memoranda, and Other Writings of John G. Nicolay, 1860–1865* (Carbondale: Southern Illinois University Press, 2000), 57. Nevins, *Frémont*, 508.

3. The Department of the West included Illinois, Missouri, Iowa, Kansas, Minnesota, Arkansas, western Kentucky, and the territories of Nebraska, Colorado, and Dakota. Michael Burlingame, *Abraham Lincoln: A Life* (Baltimore, MD: Johns Hopkins University Press, 2008), 2:201.

4. James Oakes, *Freedom National: The Destruction of Slavery in the United States, 1861–1865* (New York: W. W. Norton, 2012), 155; William Harris, *Lincoln and the Border States: Preserving the Union* (Lawrence: University Press of Kansas, 2011), 140.

5. Oakes, *Freedom National*, 148, 151–152; Harris, *Lincoln and the Border States*, 120–121.

6. Harris, *Lincoln and the Border States*, 138. The convention had originally been called in January 1861 by Governor Jackson to endorse secession, but Jackson misjudged the sentiment of the state, which voted overwhelmingly for delegates who opposed secession. The convention adjourned without taking action, but after Jackson and the pro-secessionist legislature fled the capital, Jefferson City, the convention reconvened. Oakes, *Freedom National*, 151–152.

7. Harris, *Lincoln and the Border States*, 139.

8. John C. Frémont to Abraham Lincoln, July 30, 1861, Abraham Lincoln Papers, Series 1, General Correspondence, 1833–1916, Library of Congress, http://hdl.loc.gov/loc.mss/mss00001.mss30189a.1093000, hereafter cited as ALP.

9. Harris, *Lincoln and the Border States*, 141–142; Burlingame, *Abraham Lincoln*, 2:201; Allen C. Guelzo, *Lincoln's Emancipation Proclamation: The End of Slavery in America* (New York: Simon & Schuster, 2004), 49; "Martial Law Proclaimed in St. Louis," *New York Times*, August 15, 1861. Lyon had pleaded with Frémont for reinforcements to no avail, but rather than retreat to a position he could hold, as Frémont urged, Lyon decided to launch an attack against the numerically superior enemy.

10. Oakes, *Freedom National*, 156; "Frémont's Declaration of Martial Law," August 30, 1861, *Ohio Civil War Central*, accessed June 3, 2024, https://www.ohiocivilwarcentral.com/entry.php?rec=1325.

11. Oakes, *Freedom National*, 166; Nevins, *Frémont*, 503; Pamela Herr, "Permutations of a Marriage: John Charles and Jessie Frémont's Civil War Alliance," in

Carol K. Bleser and Lesley J. Gordon, eds., *Intimate Strategies of the Civil War: Military Commanders and Their Wives* (New York: Oxford University Press, 2001), 209, 283n57.

12. Eric Foner, *The Fiery Trial: Abraham Lincoln and American Slavery* (New York: W. W. Norton, 2010), 176–177; John Fabian Witt, *Lincoln's Code: The Laws of War in American History* (New York: Free Press, 2012), 29, 72–74, 169, 199–201 (quotations at 199, 72, 169, 199).

13. Benjamin F. Butler, *Butler's Book: Autobiography and Personal Reminiscences of Major-General Benjamin Butler* (Boston: Thayer, 1892), 257; Oakes, *Freedom National*, 95–96.

14. Oakes, *Freedom National*, 96–101, quotations at 96, 99, 101.

15. Foner, *The Fiery Trial*, 174; George P. Sanger, ed., *The Statutes at Large, Treaties, and Proclamations of the United States of America*, vol. 12 (Boston: Little, Brown, 1863), 319, available electronically at https://memory.loc.gov/ammem/amlaw/lwsllink.html. A month before signing the Confiscation Act, Lincoln, according to Orville Browning, agreed that "the government neither should, nor would send back to bondage such as came to our armies" (quoted in Oakes, *Freedom National*, 112), but Lincoln also agreed, Browning added, that "we could not have them in camp, and that they must take care of themselves till the war is over, and then, colonize &c." Diary entry, July 8, 1861, in Theodore Calvin Pease and James G. Randall, eds., *The Diary of Orville Hickman Browning* (Springfield: Illinois State Historical Library, 1925), 1:478. Writing anonymously "as Lincoln's mouthpiece" in the *New York World* at the end of November 1861, Lincoln's trusted aide John Hay declared that "it is safe to assume . . . that [under the First Confiscation Act and the War Department's implementing instructions] . . . all negroes, once lawfully confiscated from the possession of their rebel owners shall become free men." This sentence is quoted as an expression of Lincoln's views by Allen Guelzo (*Lincoln's Emancipation Proclamation*, 45; also 75), but he omits Hay's next clause: ". . . leaving their future destination a matter of deliberate legislation." *Lincoln's Journalist: John Hay's Anonymous Writings for the Press, 1860–1864*, ed. Michael Burlingame (Carbondale: Southern Illinois University Press, 1998), 151. While Lincoln was determined to see that "the Negro who has once touched the hem of the government's garment shall never again be a slave"—as the president reportedly told Wendell Phillips in March 1862 (Foner, *Fiery Trial*, 197)—he seems to have been less convinced of—and committed to ensuring—the freedman's future in the United States, a theme we explore further in chapter 4.

16. Foner, *The Fiery Trial*, 175; Guelzo, *Lincoln's Emancipation Proclamation*, 45. Only one Republican in the Senate and seven in the House voted against the bill. Every member of Congress from a border state opposed the bill. Oakes, *Freedom National*, 137–138.

17. About one-fifth of Kentucky's population was enslaved, compared with about one-quarter of Tennessee's population. Slaves also made up about one-fourth of Arkansas' population. In every other Confederate state, slaves made up at least 30 percent of the population.

18. According to the 1860 census, Virginia had nearly five hundred thousand slaves and about 1.1 million free Whites. Kentucky's free population was about 930,000.

19. Lincoln to Orville Browning, September 22, 1861, in Roy P. Basler, ed., *The Collected Works of Abraham Lincoln* (New Brunswick, NJ: Rutgers University Press, 1953), 4:532. Also see Lincoln's comment in April 1861 that Kentucky "is the key to the situation." Quoted in Harris, *Lincoln and the Border States*, 80.

20. Joshua Speed to Lincoln, September 3, 1861, ALP, http://hdl.loc.gov/loc.mss/mso00001.mss30189a.1147900; Foner, *The Fiery Trial*, 177; Oakes, *Freedom National*, 159, 161; Burlingame, *Abraham Lincoln*, 2:202. Also see Joseph Holt to Lincoln, September 2, 1861, ALP, http://hdl.loc.gov/loc.mss/mso00001.mss30189a.1145100. On Kentucky's "experiment in neutrality," see Harris, *Lincoln and the Border States*, ch. 3.

21. Lincoln to Frémont, September 2, 1861, in Basler, *Collected Works*, 4:506; although dated September 2, the letter was not sent until the next day.

22. Guelzo, *Lincoln's Emancipation Proclamation*, 55; Foner, *The Fiery Trial*, 177.

23. John C. Frémont to AL, September 8, 1861 (Proclamation and situation in Missouri), ALP, http://hdl.loc.gov/loc.mss/mso00001.mss30189a.1156100. An unrepentant Frémont also disputed Lincoln's judgment about the effects of shooting captives and asked the president that he be allowed to carry out shootings "upon the spot."

24. Burlingame, *Abraham Lincoln*, 2:203; Guelzo, *Lincoln's Emancipation Proclamation*, 309n59.

25. John C. Frémont to AL, September 8, 1861 (Situation in Kentucky), ALP, http://hdl.loc.gov/loc.mss/mso00001.mss30189a.1156300.

26. Foner, *The Fiery Trial*, 177; Oakes, *Freedom National*, 153; Burlingame, *Abraham Lincoln*, 2:203; Nevins, *Frémont*, 505.

27. James M. McPherson *Battle Cry of Freedom: The Civil War Era* (New York: Oxford University Press, 1988), 353. Lincoln recalled that Jessie Frémont had "taxed me so violently with many things that I had to exercise all the awkward tact I have to avoid quarrelling with her." One member of Congress claimed that Lincoln told him that Jessie opened her case "with mild expostulation" and ended it by angrily "flaunting her handkerchief before my face and saying, 'Sir, the general will try titles with you.'" Certainly, Jessie Frémont was unimpressed with Lincoln, who she later described as having a "sly slimy nature." Burlingame, *Abraham Lincoln*, 2:205.

28. Montgomery Blair to Lincoln, September 3, 1861, ALP, http://hdl.loc.gov/loc.mss/mso00001.mss30189a.1144300. Also see Francis P. Blair Jr. to Montgomery Blair, September 1, 1861, ALP, http://hdl.loc.gov/loc.mss/mso00001.mss30189a.1143300; and Montgomery Blair to Lincoln, September 4, 1861, ALP, http://hdl.loc.gov/loc.mss/mso00001.mss30189a.1148100.

29. Lincoln to David Hunter, September 9, 1861, in Basler, *Collected Works*, 4:513. Lincoln's request followed advice offered by General Winfield Scott, who told the president that if Hunter "could be brought in close relations with . . .

Frémont some rash measures might be staved off & good ones accepted by insinuation" (4:513n).

30. Not until near the end of October, as evidence of Frémont's administrative incompetence and military ineptitude became too egregious to tolerate any longer, did Lincoln finally relieve Frémont of his command.

31. John C. Frémont to Lincoln, September 8, 1861, ALP, http://hdl.loc.gov/loc.mss/mss000001.mss30189a.1170700; Basler, *Collected Works*, 4:518n. In addition to sending the letter to Frémont, Lincoln also sent a copy to Kentucky Democrat Joseph Holt, who was desperate for the administration to disavow Frémont's emancipation order. Holt, who had served as secretary of war in the Buchanan administration, released Lincoln's letter to the papers.

32. Burlingame, *Abraham Lincoln*, 2:203. According to historian Eric Foner, Frémont's order and Lincoln's modification "inspired more letters to Lincoln than any other event of his presidency." *The Fiery Trial*, 178.

33. McPherson, *The Struggle for Equality*, 73–74.

34. Burlingame, *Abraham Lincoln*, 2:203–204; John L. Scripps to Lincoln, September 23, 1861, ALP, http://hdl.loc.gov/loc.mss/mss000001.mss30189a.1197500.

35. Writing from Indiana, Richard W. Thompson, who had served with Lincoln in Congress in the 1840s, reported that "Republicans, thus far, complain the most." Foner, *The Fiery Trial*, 181.

36. Orville Browning to Lincoln, September 17, 1861, ALP, http://hdl.loc.gov/loc.mss/mss000001.mss30189a.1172400.

37. Foner, *The Fiery Trial*, 179.

38. Lincoln to Browning, September 22, 1861, in Basler, *Collected Works*, 4:531–532.

39. Witt, *Lincoln's Code*, 197; Michael Burlingame and John R. Turner Ettlinger, eds., *Inside Lincoln's White House: The Complete Civil War Diary of John Hay* (Carbondale: Southern Illinois University Press, 1997), 20 (entry for May 7, 1861); Guelzo, *Lincoln's Emancipation Proclamation*, 59.

40. Sumner to Francis Lieber, September 17, 1861, in Beverly Wilson Palmer, ed., *The Selected Letters of Charles Sumner* (Boston: Northeastern University Press, 1990), 2:79; Guelzo, *Lincoln's Emancipation Proclamation*, 60. The importance of the legal context—the federal courts especially—in constraining Lincoln's emancipation-related decisions is a central theme in Burrus M. Carnahan, *Act of Justice: Lincoln's Emancipation Proclamation and the Law of War* (Lexington: University Press of Kentucky, 2007).

41. Foner, *The Fiery Trial*, 181; Lincoln to George Bancroft, November 18, 1861, in Basler, *Collected Works*, 5:26.

CHAPTER 2. A FAILURE TO PERSUADE

1. Clay H. Reed, "Lincoln's Compensated Emancipation Plan and Its Relation to Delaware," *Delaware Notes* 7 (1931): 33; Patience Essah, *A House Divided: Slavery and Emancipation in Delaware, 1838 to 1865* (Charlottesville: University of Virginia Press, 1996), 159.

2. "Drafts of a Bill for Compensated Emancipation in Delaware," [November 26? 1861], in Roy P. Basler, ed., *The Collected Works of Abraham Lincoln* (New Brunswick, NJ: Rutgers University Press, 1953), 5:29–30. The idea of federally compensated emancipation in the border states was hardly original to Lincoln. At the outset of the year, the *New York Tribune* endorsed a "project . . . now seriously discussed in political circles at Washington" that would "buy out all the slaves" in the border states of Delaware, Maryland, and Missouri (as well as Arkansas, Texas, and Louisiana). The *Tribune*'s editor, Horace Greeley, endorsed the plan as a "fair and reasonable compromise" and the only one that the "Free States can consent without a disgraceful sacrifice of principle, honor, and interest." Even if only a single slave state accepted the proposition, Greeley added, it "would be well worth the money." "A Reasonable Compromise" *New York Tribune*, January 16, 1861, 4. Greeley also contemplated that different schemes might be appropriate in different states. In Delaware, for instance, which had almost ten times as many free Blacks as slaves, he thought that the state "could have no serious objection to allowing her two thousand slaves to remain after emancipation as free laborers," whereas in a state like Louisiana, where slaves outnumbered Whites, the state might reasonably "prefer to have them gradually emancipated and removed to Central America, or to Haiti or Jamaica, where they would be gladly welcomed." Greeley suggested that "some definite period, not very remote, say 1876, the centennial anniversary of the Declaration of Independence, could be fixed upon as the date of final emancipation." "The Only Possible Compromise," *New York Tribune*, January 19, 1861, 6. Also see James Oakes, *Freedom National: The Destruction of Slavery in the United States, 1861–1865* (New York: W. W. Norton, 2012), 55, 288.

3. Reed, "Lincoln's Compensated Emancipation Plan," 38. The logic of Lincoln's plan was consistent with antislavery advocates' long-standing belief that the border states held the key to abolishing slavery nationwide by erecting a "cordon of freedom" around the southern states that would put slavery on what Lincoln described as "the course of ultimate extinction." Oakes, *Freedom National*, 52–54, 82, 292; James H. Read, *Sovereign of a Free People: Abraham Lincoln, Majority Rule, and Slavery* (Lawrence: University Press of Kansas, 2023), ch. 7.

4. Reed, "Lincoln's Compensated Emancipation Plan," 38. Used in a horse-drawn carriage or plough, the swingletree is a crossbar in the horse's harness, which balances the pull of the horse.

5. Charles Sumner to Wendell Phillips, December 8, 1861, in Beverly Wilson Palmer, ed., *The Selected Letters of Charles Sumner* (Boston: Northeastern University Press, 1990), 2:85.

6. Congress had convened in a special session for a month in the summer of 1861 (July 4–August 6). In the mid-nineteenth century, Congress did not begin its first regular session, which typically lasted about seven or eight months, until the December of the year after the presidential election.

7. Diary entry, December 1, 1861, in Theodore Calvin Pease and James G. Randall, eds., *The Diary of Orville Hickman Browning* (Springfield: Illinois State Historical Library, 1925), 1:512.

8. "Annual Message to Congress," December 3, 1861, in Basler, *Collected Works*, 5:48.

9. Eric Foner, *The Fiery Trial: Abraham Lincoln and American Slavery* (New York: W. W. Norton, 2010), 183; Reed, "Lincoln's Compensated Emancipation Plan," 41.

10. Reed, "Lincoln's Compensated Emancipation Plan," 42–43; Foner, *The Fiery Trial*, 184; Allen C. Guelzo, *Lincoln's Emancipation Proclamation: The End of Slavery in America* (New York: Simon & Schuster, 2004), 103.

11. Lincoln used the word "abolishment" rather than "abolition," Lincoln biographer Michael Burlingame surmises, because the former was a term "less likely to raise conservative hackles than *abolition*." Michael Burlingame, *Abraham Lincoln: A Life* (Baltimore, MD: Johns Hopkins University Press, 2008), 2:335, emphasis in original.

12. "Message to Congress," March 5, 1862, in Basler, *Collected Works*, 5:144–146.

13. Foner, *The Fiery Trial*, 196; Burlingame, *Abraham Lincoln*, 2:336–339; William Harris, *Lincoln and the Border States: Preserving the Union* (Lawrence: University Press of Kansas, 2011), 165.

14. Burlingame, *Abraham Lincoln*, 2:339; Journal entry, March 9, 1862, in Michael Burlingame, ed., *With Lincoln in the White House: Letters, Memoranda, and Other Writings of John G. Nicolay, 1860–1865* (Carbondale: Southern Illinois University Press, 2000), 73–74.

15. Burlingame, *Abraham Lincoln*, 2:342–343; Foner, *The Fiery Trial*, 197; Guelzo, *Lincoln's Emancipation Proclamation*, 106.

16. The House approved the resolution in the second week of March, the Senate on April 2, and Lincoln signed it on April 10. The vote was 89–31 in the House and 32–10 in the Senate. Guelzo, *Lincoln's Emancipation Proclamation*, 49. The day after the Senate passed the joint resolution, it passed a bill requiring the immediate, compensated emancipation of all slaves in the nation's capital. The House approved the measure on April 12, and Lincoln signed the act into law on April 16. The legislation not only compensated slaveowners up to $300 for each slave but also provided $100,000 to support the voluntary emigration of freed Blacks in the District of Columbia. The latter provision was introduced by Wisconsin senator and close Lincoln ally James Doolittle as a substitute to an amendment offered by Kentucky senator Garrett Davis that would have made colonization compulsory for those freed by the act. Lincoln's involvement in the legislative deliberations was minimal, and he was far from enthusiastic about the Senate bill because he feared abolition of slavery in the District of Columbia would increase opposition to his border state plan. He was also not happy that the bill required immediate rather than gradual emancipation and that it made no provision for a popular vote to ratify the measure. Despite his misgivings, he ultimately signed the bill, singling out for praise Congress's decision to incorporate "the two principles of compensation and colonization." The compensation provision worked largely as planned, as hundreds of slaveholders were paid about $900,000 to compensate for the roughly three thousand slaves freed by the act. The colonization provi-

sion, in contrast, failed miserably, as DC's fourteen thousand Black residents showed limited interest in leaving the country, and the government did not have a viable plan of where to send those who were willing to leave. Foner, *The Fiery Trial*, 199–201.

17. Foner, *The Fiery Trial*, 197–198; Burlingame, *Abraham Lincoln*, 2:343.

18. Harris, *Lincoln and the Border States*, 188; Foner, *The Fiery Trial*, 198.

19. Guelzo, *Lincoln's Emancipation Proclamation*, 115, 107.

20. "Proclamation Revoking General Hunter's Order of Military Emancipation of May 9, 1862," May 19, 1862, in Basler, *Collected Works*, 5:223. On Hunter, "one of the few abolitionists in the officer corps" (Foner, *Fiery Trial*, 206), see Edward A. Miller Jr., *Lincoln's Abolitionist General: The Biography of David Hunter* (Columbia: University of South Carolina Press, 1997).

21. Louis Masur, *Lincoln's Hundred Days: The Emancipation Proclamation and the War for the Union* (Cambridge, MA: Harvard University Press, 2012), 58.

22. Gideon Welles, "History of Emancipation," in Albert Mordell, ed., *Civil War and Reconstruction: Selected Essays by Gideon Welles* (New York: Twayne Publishers, 1959), 236; Guelzo, *Lincoln's Emancipation Proclamation*, 120.

23. Welles, "History of Emancipation," 236; "Appeal to Border State Representatives to Favor Compensated Emancipation," July 12, 1862, in Basler, *Collected Works*, 5:317.

24. Masur, *Lincoln's Hundred Days*, 71.

25. "Appeal to Border State Representatives," in Basler, *Collected Works*, 5:317–318; Richard E. Neustadt, *Presidential Power: The Politics of Leadership* (New York: Wiley, 1960), 46.

26. "Appeal to Border State Representatives," in Basler, *Collected Works*, 5:318, emphasis in original.

27. "Appeal to Border State Representatives," 5:318. Lincoln had hinted at wielding this power for the first time in his proclamation revoking Hunter's emancipation order, in which he declared that the judgment as to "whether ... it shall have become a necessity indispensable to the maintenance of the government ... to declare the Slaves of any state or states, free" was his alone to make as the "Commander-in-Chief of the Army and Navy." "Proclamation Revoking General Hunter's Order of Military Emancipation," 5:222. Also see Foner, *Fiery Trial*, 207; and Salmon Chase to Benjamin Butler, June 24, 1862, *The Salmon Chase Papers*, ed. John Niven (Kent, OH: Kent State University Press, 1996), 3:219.

28. "Appeal to Border State Representatives," in Basler, *Collected Works*, 5:319; Guelzo, *Lincoln's Emancipation Proclamation*, 122.

29. Guelzo, *Lincoln's Emancipation Proclamation*, 122; Border State Congressmen to Abraham Lincoln, July 14, 1862, Abraham Lincoln Papers, Series 1, General Correspondence, 1833–1916, Library of Congress, http://hdl.loc.gov/loc.mss/mss00001.mss30189a.1708800, hereafter cited as ALP. Nine of the twenty signatories represented Kentucky, five represented Missouri, five represented Maryland, and one was from Virginia (soon to be West Virginia); three were US senators and the rest were House members. A minority reply, issued July 15, 1862

(http://hdl.loc.gov/loc.mss/mss00001.mss30189a.1713000), was signed by six US House members and one senator, but only one representative from Kentucky, one from Missouri, and none from Maryland; the others were George Fisher, Delaware's sole representative in the House, two Virginia House members and one Virginia senator, and one Tennessee House member—another Tennessee member replied the following day supporting Lincoln's appeal. Basler, *Collected Works*, 5:319n. The other border state representatives, including most of the senators from these states, including both senators from Delaware and Maryland, did not even bother to show up for let alone respond to Lincoln's reading of his address.

30. Border State Congressmen to Abraham Lincoln, July 14, 1862, ALP.
31. Welles, "History of Emancipation," 253, 238.
32. Noah Feldman, *The Broken Constitution: Lincoln, Slavery, and the Refounding of America* (New York: Farrar, Straus & Giroux, 2021), 262; Harris, *Lincoln and the Border States*, 188.
33. "To the Senate and the House of Representatives," July 14, 1862, in Basler, *Collected Works*, 5:324.
34. Sen. Jacob Collamer, quoted in Burlingame, *Abraham Lincoln*, 2:356.

CHAPTER 3. A PAINFUL LAST RESORT

1. Allen C. Guelzo, *Lincoln's Emancipation Proclamation: The End of Slavery in America* (New York: Simon & Schuster, 2004), 125. The act emerged from the conference committee on July 12, the same day that Lincoln met with the border state representatives.
2. James Oakes, *Freedom National: The Destruction of Slavery in the United States, 1861–1865* (New York: W. W. Norton 2012), 239.
3. Oakes, *Freedom National*, 240. Diary entry, July 14, 1862, in Theodore Calvin Pease and James G. Randall, eds., *The Diary of Orville Hickman Browning* (Springfield: Illinois State Historical Library, 1925), 1:558. Also see the letter to Lincoln from Marylander Anna Ella Carroll, July 14, 1862, Abraham Lincoln Papers, Series 1, General Correspondence, 1833–1916, Library of Congress, http://hdl.loc.gov/loc.mss/mss00001.mss30189a.1704800, hereafter cited as ALP.
4. Noah Feldman, *The Broken Constitution: Lincoln, Slavery, and the Refounding of America* (New York: Farrar, Straus & Giroux, 2021), 261–262. This was hardly the first time Lincoln had heard this argument. See, for instance, the letter to Lincoln from Elihu Burritt, June 2, 1862, ALP, http://hdl.loc.gov/loc.mss/mss00001.mss30189a.1626700. Also see the letter of the same date from the veteran Whig politician and lawyer from Ohio, Thomas Ewing (who in 1868 would be Andrew Johnson's ill-fated choice to replace the fired Edwin Stanton as secretary of war), ALP, http://hdl.loc.gov/loc.mss/mss00001.mss30189a.1627200. These same arguments had also been considered at the time of the First Confiscation Act and were part of why Lincoln had been reluctant to sign that legislation. The reality, though, was that the act relied on such a "cumbersome judicial process" that it resulted in little land ever being seized let alone sold. Eric Foner,

The Fiery Trial: Abraham Lincoln and American Slavery (New York: W. W. Norton, 2010), 215.

5. Guelzo, *Lincoln's Emancipation Proclamation*, 72, 127, 45. Also see John Syrett, *The Civil War Confiscation Acts: Failing to Reconstruct the South* (New York: Fordham University Press, 2005), 55.

6. "Sterner Measures Demanded: An Emphatic Letter from Gov. [Richard] Yates of Illinois to Mr. Lincoln, July 11, 1862," *New York Times*, July 20, 1862; Foner, *The Fiery Trial*, 216. Also see Michael Burlingame, *Abraham Lincoln: A Life* (Baltimore, MD: Johns Hopkins University Press, 2008), 2:365; and Oakes, *Freedom National*, 242–243.

7. Diary entry, July 15, 1862, in Pease and Randall, *Diary of Browning*, 1:559–560.

8. Burlingame, *Abraham Lincoln*, 2:358–359.

9. William E. Gienapp and Erica L. Gienapp, eds., *Civil War Diary of Gideon Welles, Lincoln's Secretary of the Navy* (Urbana: University of Illinois Press, 2014), 3–4. The conversation that Welles related took place on a carriage ride to the funeral of Stanton's infant son; Seward and his wife were also in the carriage.

10. Guelzo, *Lincoln's Emancipation Proclamation*, 151.

11. "Emancipation Proclamation—First Draft," [July 22, 1862], in Roy P. Basler, ed., *The Collected Works of Abraham Lincoln* (New Brunswick, NJ: Rutgers University Press, 1953), 5:336–337. Chase's lack of enthusiasm for the proclamation must have surprised Lincoln since Chase had lobbied for sustaining Hunter's proclamation of emancipation in May. And only a month before the cabinet meeting, Chase had expressed his hope that the president would soon "recognize the same necessity" that he did of using "the war power [to] destroy slavery." Chase to Benjamin Butler, June 24, 1862, in John Niven, ed., *The Salmon Chase Papers* (Kent, OH: Kent State University Press, 1996), 3:219.

12. Guelzo, *Lincoln's Emancipation Proclamation*, 134–136.

13. Guelzo, 137. Also see Louis Masur, *Lincoln's Hundred Days: The Emancipation Proclamation and the War for the Union* (Cambridge, MA: Harvard University Press, 2012), 82–83.

14. Guelzo, *Lincoln's Emancipation Proclamation*, 137. Also see Masur, *Lincoln's Hundred Days*, 83. Weed's message that the proclamation "would work no good and probably would do much harm" (Guelzo, 157) was echoed by James Speed, an antislavery Kentuckian (and brother of Lincoln's close friend Joshua Speed), whose judgment Lincoln trusted and to whom he had read a draft of the proclamation. In a letter dated July 28, 1862, Speed reported to Lincoln, "The more I have thought of it, the more I am satisfied that [the proclamation] will do no good; most probably much harm." "A sweeping proclamation," Speed continued, "would be idle because impracticable—It would but delude the poor negro, and shock most violently the prejudices of many in the north & nearly all in the South." James Speed to Lincoln, July 28, 1862, ALP, http://hdl.loc.gov/loc.mss/mss000001.mss30189a.1731600.

15. Lincoln to Reverdy Johnson, July 26, 1862, in Basler, *Collected Works*, 5:343; Masur, *Lincoln's Hundred Days*, 83; "Emancipation Proclamation—First Draft,"

5:336–337. The day after issuing the "Proclamation of the Act to Suppress Insurrection" (July 25, 1862, in Basler, *Collected Works*, 5:341), shorn of the proclamation of emancipation, Lincoln vented some of his frustrations to Reverdy Johnson, a Democrat who had played an important role in keeping Maryland loyal to the Union. The "appeal of professed friends," Lincoln complained, "has paralyzed me more in this struggle than any other thing," but he insisted that he would "not surrender this game, leaving any available card unplayed" (5:343). On the persistence of Lincoln's reservations about the wisdom of the proclamation into the fall of 1862, see Burlingame, *Abraham Lincoln*, 2:422.

CHAPTER 4. A FAILURE TO PERSUADE (AGAIN)

1. Lincoln to Horace Greeley, August 22, 1862, in Roy P. Basler, ed., *The Collected Works of Abraham Lincoln* (New Brunswick, NJ: Rutgers University Press, 1953), 5:388, emphasis in original.

2. Michael Burlingame, *Abraham Lincoln: A Life* (Baltimore, MD: Johns Hopkins University Press, 2008), 2:335; Eric Foner, *The Fiery Trial: Abraham Lincoln and American Slavery* (New York: W. W. Norton, 2010), 198–199; William Harris, *Lincoln and the Border States: Preserving the Union* (Lawrence: University Press of Kansas, 2011), 173.

3. John P. Usher to Abraham Lincoln, August 2, 1862, Abraham Lincoln Papers, Series 1, General Correspondence, 1833–1916, Library of Congress, http://hdl.loc.gov/loc.mss/ms000001.mss30189a.1742700, hereafter cited as ALP. Usher also predicted that the plan would "alarm those in rebellion, for they will see that their cherished property is departing from them forever and incline them to peace," which paralleled the argument Lincoln had been making for gradual emancipation in the border states.

4. As Kate Masur notes, Mitchell "was hardly the kind of figure who inspired trust among African Americans." Kate Masur, "The African American Delegation to Abraham Lincoln: A Reappraisal," *Civil War History* 56, no. 2 (June 2010): 129. Long active in colonization efforts, Mitchell published a report on colonization in May 1862, addressed to Lincoln, in which he warned of a coming race war, compared to which the Civil War, he said, would look "moderate and altogether tolerable" (3). The danger, Mitchell explained, was that "we have 4,500,000 persons, who, whilst amongst us, cannot be of us—persons of a different race, forming necessarily a different interest; the germ of a distinct political power, not now fully disclosed, but to be disclosed in future ages" (4). He warned that the White majority would "never submit" (10) to the most "repulsive admixture of blood" that would result from "pour[ing] the blood of near five million Africans into the veins of the Republic" (8). James Mitchell to Abraham Lincoln, May 18, 1862, "Letter on the Relation of the White and African Races in the United States, Showing the Necessity of the Colonization of the Latter," addressed to the president of the US (Washington, DC: Government Printing Office, 1862), ALP, http://hdl.loc.gov/loc.mss/ms000001.mss30189a.1604400. On Mitchell and his connec-

tions to Lincoln, see Mark E. Neely Jr., "Colonization and the Myth that Lincoln Prepared the People for Emancipation," in *Lincoln's Proclamation: Emancipation Reconsidered*, ed. William A. Blair and Karen Fisher Younger (Chapel Hill: University of North Carolina Press, 2009), 58–63; Mark E. Neely Jr., *Lincoln and the Triumph of the Nation: Constitutional Conflict in the American Civil War* (Chapel Hill: University of North Carolina Press, 2011), 118–119; and Michael Burlingame, *The Black Man's President: Abraham Lincoln, African Americans, and the Pursuit of Racial Equality* (New York: Pegasus, 2021), 58. Also see Lincoln's letter to William H. Seward, October 3, 1861, in Basler, *Collected Works*, 4:547 ("Mitchell . . . I know and like . . . ").

5. Foner, *The Fiery Trial*, 223–224; Burlingame, *The Black Man's President*, 51–56, 58–59; Masur, "The African American Delegation to Abraham Lincoln," 128.

6. Burlingame, *The Black Man's President*, 71; Masur, "The African American Delegation to Abraham Lincoln," 130.

7. Burlingame, *The Black Man's President*, 60–64; "Address on Colonization to a Deputation of Negroes," August 14, 1862, in Basler, *Collected Works*, 5:371–372.

8. Lincoln, "Address on Colonization," in Basler, *Collected Works*, 5:372–373.

9. "Address on Colonization," 5:373–374.

10. "Address on Colonization," 5:375.

11. Thomas asked the president for funds to cover his trip to solicit support for colonization, which Thomas assured him would, within a few weeks, lead to the "active and zealous Support of this measure." Edward M. Thomas to Lincoln, August 16, 1862, ALP, http://hdl.loc.gov/loc.mss/mss00001.mss30189a.1771800. Thomas did make the trip, but it was funded not out of the colonization funds appropriated by Congress but by Jacob Van Vleet, the editor of Washington's *National Republican*, who had been instrumental in getting the Union Bethel gathering to send a delegation to meet with Lincoln. Masur, "The African American Delegation to Abraham Lincoln," 137.

12. Masur, 135.

13. Foner, *The Fiery Trial*, 224–226; James Oakes, *Freedom National: The Destruction of Slavery in the United States, 1861–1865* (New York: W. W. Norton 2012), 310; Burlingame, *Abraham Lincoln*, 2:390; Noah Feldman, *The Broken Constitution: Lincoln, Slavery, and the Refounding of America* (New York: Farrar, Straus & Giroux, 2021), 274. So offensive did Douglass find Lincoln's formulation that he returned to it years later in his famous oration at the unveiling of the Emancipation Memorial in Lincoln Park, recalling the day when Lincoln "strangely told us that we were the cause of the war."

14. Foner, *The Fiery Trial*, 225–226; Burlingame, *The Black Man's President*, 65, 100; Masur, "The African American Delegation to Abraham Lincoln," 138–139. Pomeroy, who had been an opponent of colonization (Burlingame, *Abraham Lincoln*, 2:392–393), was a much better choice than Mitchell as "the public face of [the president's] colonization policy" (Masur, "The African American Delegation to Abraham Lincoln," 138). Unlike the deeply racist Mitchell, for whom colonization was a way of avoiding the "admixture of blood," Pomeroy focused his case for

colonization on Black empowerment: "Let us plant you free and independent beyond the reach of the power that has oppressed you," Pomeroy urged in his recruitment appeal, "To the Free Colored People of the United States" (138; also see Burlingame, *Abraham Lincoln*, 2:393). It is not clear how Lincoln prevailed on Pomeroy to spearhead the colonization effort—we know Lincoln met with Pomeroy "at length" (Foner, *The Fiery Trial*, 225, 226) shortly after his August 14th meeting with the delegation of Blacks—but he seems to have dangled emancipation as a carrot, vowing to Pomeroy that "he would emancipate as soon as he was assured that his colonization project would succeed." Burlingame, *Abraham Lincoln*, 2:383. Burlingame speculates that it's also possible that Pomeroy, a famously "shady character" who would become the model for a corrupt senator in Mark Twain's *The Gilded Age*, saw Chiriquí as a money-making scheme. Burlingame, *Abraham Lincoln*, 2:393.

15. Burlingame, *Abraham Lincoln*, 2:394; Burlingame, *The Black Man's President*, 100; Foner, *The Fiery Trial*, 233–234.

16. Welles, quoted in Burlingame, *Abraham Lincoln*, 2:392.

17. Burlingame, *Abraham Lincoln*, 2:391. Also see the *New York Times*, quoted in Neely, "Colonization and the Myth," 54.

18. Burlingame, *The Black Man's President*, 64–56; Feldman, *The Broken Constitution*, 272; Lincoln, "Address on Colonization," in Basler, *Collected Works*, 5:372; Masur, "The African American Delegation to Abraham Lincoln," 138; Foner, *The Fiery Trial*, 226.

19. Richard E. Neustadt, *Presidential Power: The Politics of Leadership* (New York: Wiley, 1960), 32; Frederick Douglass, "An 1876 Speech Given by Frederick Douglass at the Unveiling of the Freedmen's Monument in Lincoln Park, Washington, DC," Digital Public Library of America, accessed June 7, 2024, https://dp.la/primary-source-sets/frederick-douglass-and-abraham-lincoln/sources/104; Burlingame, *Abraham Lincoln*, 2:390 (quoting William Catto). Douglas's speech is analyzed in Burlingame, *The Black Man's President*, 193–199.

20. Burlingame, *The Black Man's President*, 60–64; Neely, "Colonization and the Myth," 55–56.

CHAPTER 5. "THE TIME HAS COME NOW"

1. For an in-depth analysis of this episode, see Richard Carwardine, "Whatever Shall Appear to be God's Will, I Will Do: The Chicago Initiative and Lincoln's Proclamation," in *Lincoln's Proclamation: Emancipation Reconsidered*, ed. William A. Blair and Karen Fisher Younger (Chapel Hill: University of North Carolina Press, 2009), 75–101. Also see Paul Finkelman, "The President and the Pastors," *New York Times*, September 21, 2012.

2. "Reply to Emancipation Memorial Presented by Chicago Christians of all Denominations," September 13, 1862, in Roy P. Basler, ed., *The Collected Works of Abraham Lincoln* (New Brunswick, NJ: Rutgers University Press, 1953), 5:422–424.

3. "Reply to Emancipation Memorial," in Basler, *Collected Works*, 5:419–421,

423–424; "Meditation on the Divine Will," [September 2, 1862?], in Basler, *Collected Works*, 5:403–404. Lincoln expressed this same skepticism many times. See "Remarks to a Delegation of Progressive Friends," June 20, 1862, in Basler, *Collected Works*, 5:279; and his comments to a delegation of abolitionist ministers on December 31, 1862, in Worth Brown and Randolph C. Downes, "A Conference with Abraham Lincoln, from the diary of Reverend Nathan Brown," *Northwest Ohio Quarterly* 22 (1950): 59, https://toledosattic.org/images/pdfs/nwoq-by-issue/NWOQ_1950_Vol22-2.pdf.

4. "Reply to Emancipation Memorial," in Basler, *Collected Works*, 5:425, 420. Lincoln's comments echoed what he told another group of visitors a few months before: "If a decree of emancipation could abolish Slavery, John Brown would have done the work effectually. Such a decree surely could not be more binding upon the South than the Constitution, and that cannot be enforced in that part of the country now. Would a proclamation of freedom be any more effective?" "Remarks to a Delegation of Progressive Friends," in Basler, *Collected Works*, 5:278. Also see John Hay's explanation of Lincoln's thinking about the limits of unilateral directives: "While the contest could be carried on without an executive pronunciamento, the President thought best to keep silent." Michael Burlingame, ed., *Lincoln's Journalist: John Hay's Anonymous Writings for the Press, 1860–1864* (Carbondale: Southern Illinois University Press, 1998), 308 (September 22, 1862).

5. "Reply to Emancipation Memorial," in Basler, *Collected Works*, 5:420–421, 423–425.

6. Diary entry of September 16, 1862, in William E. Gienapp and Erica L. Gienapp, eds., *Civil War Diary of Gideon Welles, Lincoln's Secretary of the Navy* (Urbana: University of Illinois Press, 2014), 46; Frances Carpenter, *The Inner Life of Abraham Lincoln: Six Months at the White House* (Lincoln: University of Nebraska Press, 1985), 22; Basler, *Collected Works*, 5:404n; Louis Masur, *Lincoln's Hundred Days: The Emancipation Proclamation and the War for the Union* (Cambridge, MA: Harvard University Press, 2012), 92–93. Also see Michael Burlingame, *Abraham Lincoln: A Life* (Baltimore, MD: Johns Hopkins University Press, 2008), 2:375.

7. Diary entry of September 5, 1862, in Michael Burlingame and John R. Turner Ettlinger, eds., *Inside Lincoln's White House: The Complete Civil War Diary of John Hay* (Carbondale: Southern Illinois University Press, 1997), 39; diary entries of September 7 and 2, 1862, in Gienapp and Gienapp, *Diary of Gideon Welles*, 32, 27; Allen C. Guelzo, *Lincoln's Emancipation Proclamation: The End of Slavery in America* (New York: Simon & Schuster, 2004), 164; Burlingame, *Abraham Lincoln*, 2:376–377.

8. Diary entry of September 16, 1862, in Gienapp and Gienapp, *Diary of Gideon Welles*, 45; George Templeton Strong, diary entry of August 4, 1862, quoted in Douglas L. Wilson, *Lincoln's Sword: The Presidency and the Power of Words* (New York: Vintage, 2006), 148; Zachariah Chandler to Lyman Trumbull, September 10, 1862, quoted in Guelzo, *Lincoln's Emancipation Proclamation*, 163. Also see Eric

Foner, *The Fiery Trial: Abraham Lincoln and American Slavery* (New York: W. W. Norton, 2010), 226–227.

9. Mark E. Neely Jr., *Lincoln and the Triumph of the Nation: Constitutional Conflict in the American Civil War* (Chapel Hill: University of North Carolina Press, 2011), 127; diary entry of September 22, 1862, in David Donald, ed., *Inside Lincoln's Cabinet: The Civil War Diaries of Salmon P. Chase* (New York: Longmans, 1954), 150–151; Guelzo, *Lincoln's Emancipation Proclamation*, 171.

10. Burlingame, *Abraham Lincoln*, 2:380–383; James Oakes, *Freedom National: The Destruction of Slavery in the United States, 1861–1865* (New York: W. W. Norton 2012), 314; Donald, *Inside Lincoln's Cabinet*, 150.

11. Donald, *Inside Lincoln's Cabinet*, 150; Gienapp and Gienapp, *Diary of Gideon Welles*, 54; Guelzo, *Lincoln's Emancipation Proclamation*, 169. Also see William O. Stoddard, *Inside the White House in War Times: Memoirs and Reports of Lincoln's Secretary*, ed. Michael Burlingame (Lincoln: University of Nebraska Press, 2000), 95.

12. "Preliminary Emancipation Proclamation," September 22, 1862, in Basler, *Collected Works*, 5:434; Foner, *The Fiery Trial*, 231.

13. "Preliminary Emancipation Proclamation," in Basler, *Collected Works*, 5:434. Seward succeeded in adding a final clause, "with the previously obtained consent of the Governments existing there" (5:434n).

14. Lincoln's claim to have placed the decision in God's hands was a bit disingenuous, since, as he later admitted, he fully "expected [Lee] would do it sometime or other." Guelzo, *Lincoln's Emancipation Proclamation*, 169.

15. Oakes, *Freedom National*, 329.

16. Foner, *The Fiery Trial*, 228, 231; Masur, *Lincoln's Hundred Days*, 96, 309n38.

17. Oakes, *Freedom National*, 308; Horace Greeley, "A Prayer of Twenty Millions," *New York Tribune*, August 20, 1862, https://www.americanantiquarian.org/Manuscripts/greeley.html; Mark E. Neely Jr., "Colonization and the Myth that Lincoln Prepared the People for Emancipation," in *Lincoln's Proclamation*, 66–67. *Chicago Tribune*, August 27, 1862, quoted in Foner, *The Fiery Trial*, 230.

18. Burlingame, *Abraham Lincoln*, 2:409; Gienapp and Gienapp, *Diary of Gideon Welles*, 54; Donald, *Inside Lincoln's Cabinet*, 152.

19. Burlingame, *Abraham Lincoln*, 2:409; Gienapp and Gienapp, *Diary of Gideon Welles*, 54; Masur, *Lincoln's Hundred Days*, 146.

20. Wilson, *Lincoln's Sword*, 160. In his diary on September 22, 1862, Gideon Welles wrote, "The effect which the Proclamation will have on the public mind is a matter of some uncertainty." Gienapp and Gienapp, *Diary of Gideon Welles*, 55. Historian James Oakes contends that while Lincoln was waiting for the people to be "educated up" to support other policies, such as the arming of Black troops, "he never made that claim about emancipation." Oakes, *Freedom National*, 533n13. In fact, however, the "educated up to it" quote that is attributed to Lincoln by John McClintock clearly refers to the preliminary emancipation proclamation, which did not include arming Black troops: "When I issued that proclamation," Lincoln told McClintock, "I was in great doubt about it myself. I did not think

that public had been quite educated up to it, and I feared its effects upon the border states." Don Fehrenbacher and Virginia Fehrenbacher, eds., *Recollected Words of Abraham Lincoln* (Stanford, CA: Stanford University Press, 1996), 314. More important, there is plenty of other evidence regarding Lincoln's doubts about public support for emancipation. For instance, in a White House meeting with a group of prominent abolitionists, including Wendell Phillips, Moncure Conway, and Elizur Wright, on January 25, 1863, Lincoln was adamant that "he did not believe that his administration would have been supported by the country in a policy of emancipation at any earlier stage of the war." He also told them that "he did not believe that the Northern people as a whole regarded [Frémont's] proclamation with favor." Moncure Daniel Conway, *Autobiography, Memories and Experience* (London: Cassell, 1904), 1:338. Oakes's claim that "there is abundant evidence that emancipation was widely popular among Republicans from the very start of the war" (Oakes, *Freedom National*, 534n13) may be true but it elides that Lincoln's concern was not with Republicans only but with "the Northern people as a whole." As Lincoln reminded the abolitionists, "he had been elected by a minority of the people," which meant he could ill afford to consult only the wishes of his own partisans. Conway, *Autobiography*, 1:338.

21. Toward the end of August, Lincoln reportedly told a close friend, Congressman Isaac Arnold, that "the meaning of his letter to Greeley was . . . that he was ready to declare emancipation when he was convinced that it could be made effective and that the people were with him." Adam S. Hill to Sydney Howard Gay, September 1, 1862, quoted in Burlingame, *Abraham Lincoln*, 2:402; and Wilson, *Lincoln's Sword*, 160.

22. "It might be thought strange," Lincoln confessed to his cabinet, "but there were times [,] when he felt uncertain how to act . . . [and] when the way was not clear to his mind what he should do," that he "submitted the disposal of matters . . . in this way." Gienapp and Gienapp, *Diary of Gideon Welles*, 54.

23. Foner, *The Fiery Trial*, 231.

24. "Preliminary Emancipation Proclamation," in Basler, *Collected Works*, 5:433–436; Oakes, *Freedom National*, 335.

25. Donald, *Inside Lincoln's Cabinet*, 152. At the meeting, Blair initially indicated a desire to have his objections formally entered in the record but later decided "he would not file them, lest they should be subject to misconstruction," since he objected only to the timing of the proclamation and not its content. Hay, Diary entry of September 24, 1862, in Burlingame and Ettlinger, *Inside Lincoln's White House*, 40.

26. In making this claim, Lincoln was not staking out new ground but rather affirming Republican orthodoxy that distinguished sharply between the "object" or "purpose" of the war—suppressing the rebellion and restoring the Union—and the means used to win the war, which might require emancipation (as well as the effects of the war, which might result in emancipation). In the previous summer's congressional debates leading up to passage of the First Confiscation Act, even a quintessential Republican moderate like Ohio's John Sherman conceded

that if there was "no way of conquering South Carolina, for instance, except by emancipating her slaves, I say emancipate her slaves and conquer her rebellious citizens." And even a Republican as radical as Thaddeus Stevens, who "made the strongest case for emancipation under the laws of war," allowed that "our object is to subdue the rebels." Oakes, *Freedom National*, 115, 128, 136.

27. Wilson, *Lincoln's Sword*, 145, 151; Lincoln to Horace Greeley, in Basler, *Collected Works*, August 22, 1862, 5:388. Also see Foner, *Fiery Trial*, 229. As Wilson shows, the substantive core of Lincoln's public "reply" was written before Greeley's letter was published (Wilson, *Lincoln's Sword*, 149) and was not really a direct answer to Greeley's criticisms, as Greeley was quick to recognize (Burlingame, *Abraham Lincoln*, 2:403). Wilson argues that Lincoln seized on Greeley's letter as an opportune moment to publish something he had been eager to inject into the public dialogue around emancipation. In contrast, Mark Neely sees it as evidence that Greeley's letter, which itself may have been prompted by a leak from the cabinet, forced Lincoln to rush the letter prematurely "into the public well before any possible military victory was in sight." Neely, "Colonization and the Myth," 67.

28. Thurlow Weed to William H. Seward, August 23, 1862; John B. Henderson to Abraham Lincoln, September 3, 1862; Wendell Phillips to Sydney Howard Gay, September 2, 1862; Sydney Howard Gay to Lincoln, [August 1862], all quoted in Burlingame, *Abraham Lincoln*, 2:402. Also see Oakes, *Freedom National*, 312. An incensed Phillips added, "If the proclamation of Emanc[ipation] is possible at any time from Lincoln (which I somewhat doubt) it will be wrung from him only by fear. He's a Spaniel by nature—nothing broad, generous, or highhearted about him." Burlingame, *Abraham Lincoln*, 2:402.

29. In *Lincoln's Sword*, Douglas L. Wilson comes to a very different conclusion, declaring that "there could be little doubt that the Greeley letter had helped enormously in the process of educating the public up to the point of emancipation" (160). However, while Wilson's masterful analysis of the composition of the letter expertly unpacks Lincoln's words and his intentions, it provides little evidence to support his claim about the letter's *impact* on its audience.

30. Oakes, *Freedom National*, 312, 310; Neely, *Lincoln and the Triumph of the Nation*, 127. Frederick Douglass was hardly the only abolitionist to worry that Lincoln's colonization message left "less ground to hope for anti-slavery action at his hands than any of his previous utterances." "The President and His Speeches," *Douglass Monthly*, September 1862, 708.

31. Robert Dale Owen to Edwin M. Stanton, July 23, 1862, quoted in Oakes, *Freedom National*, 331. Oakes observes that "federal antislavery policy seemed to progress most rapidly when Union armies fared most poorly" (394).

32. Neely, *Lincoln and the Triumph of the Nation*, 131. Neely concludes that "Lincoln could have hardly done a poorer job of managing the news of the Emancipation Proclamation" (127).

33. Lincoln to Albert G. Hodges, April 4, 1864, in Basler, *Collected Works*, 7:282; Richard E. Neustadt, *Presidential Power: The Politics of Leadership* (New York: Wiley, 1960), 11.

CHAPTER 6. THE COST OF COMMAND

1. Louis Masur, *Lincoln's Hundred Days: The Emancipation Proclamation and the War for the Union* (Cambridge, MA: Harvard University Press, 2012), 103, 113; Allen C. Guelzo, *Lincoln's Emancipation Proclamation: The End of Slavery in America* (New York: Simon & Schuster, 2004), 178–180.

2. Masur, *Lincoln's Hundred Days*, 103, 114.

3. Lincoln to Hannibal Hamlin, September 28, 1862, in Roy P. Basler, ed., *The Collected Works of Abraham Lincoln* (New Brunswick, NJ: Rutgers University Press, 1953), 5:444. Hamlin's letter to the president was written on September 25.

4. Jacob Dolson Cox, *Military Reminiscences of the Civil War*, 2 vols. (New York: Charles Scribner's Sons, 1900), 1:355; Record of Dismissal of John J. Key, September 26–27, 1862, and Lincoln to John J. Key, November 24, 1862, in Basler, *Collected Works*, 5:442, 508; Michael Burlingame and John R. Turner Ettlinger, eds., *Inside Lincoln's White House: The Complete Civil War Diary of John Hay* (Carbondale: Southern Illinois University Press, 1997), 232; Guelzo, *Lincoln's Emancipation Proclamation*, 183–184; Jonathan W. White, *Emancipation, the Union Army, and the Reelection of Abraham Lincoln* (Baton Rouge: Louisiana State University Press, 2014), 43.

5. Guelzo, *Lincoln's Emancipation Proclamation*, 183–184; McClellan to Mary Ellen McClellan, September 25, 1862, and McClellan to William H. Aspinwall, September 26, 1862, in Stephen W. Sears, ed., *The Civil War Papers of George B. McClellan: Selected Correspondence, 1860–1865* (New York: Ticknor & Fields, 1989), 481–482.

6. Cox, *Military Reminiscences of the Civil War*, 1:359–360; McClellan to Mary Ellen McClellan, October 5, 1862, in Sears, *Civil War Papers*, 490.

7. Guelzo, *Lincoln's Emancipation Proclamation*, 186; Cox, *Military Reminiscences of the Civil War*, 1:361–362.

8. Guelzo, *Lincoln's Emancipation Proclamation*, 183, 187.

9. Not until 1872 did Congress pass a law requiring that all congressional elections be held on the same day in November of even-numbered years. See Michael F. Holt, "Change and Continuity in the Party Period: The Substance and Structure of American Politics, 1835–1885," in *Contesting Democracy: Substance and Structure in American Political History, 1775–2000*, ed. Byron E. Shafer and Anthony J. Badger (Lawrence: University Press of Kansas, 2001), 102.

10. All congressional results from the 37th and 38th Congress are from Michael J. Dubin, *United States Congressional Elections, 1788–1997* (Jefferson, NC: McFarland, 1998). All gubernatorial results are from Michael J. Dubin, *United States Gubernatorial Elections, 1776–1860* (Jefferson, NC: McFarland, 2003); and Michael J. Dubin, *United States Gubernatorial Elections, 1861–1911* (Jefferson, NC: McFarland, 2010).

11. Guelzo, *Lincoln's Emancipation Proclamation*, 187; Mark E. Neely Jr., *Lincoln and the Triumph of the Nation: Constitutional Conflict in the American Civil War* (Chapel Hill: University of North Carolina Press, 2011), 128.

12. Diary entry of October 5, 1862, in David Donald, ed., *Inside Lincoln's Cab-*

inet: The Civil War Diaries of Salmon P. Chase (New York: Longmans, 1954), 167; John Sherman to Chase, September 28, 1862, in John Niven, ed., *The Salmon Chase Papers* (Kent, OH: Kent State University Press, 1996), 3:287.

13. John Nicolay to Therena Bates, October 16, 1862, in Michael Burlingame, ed., *With Lincoln in the White House: Letters, Memoranda, and Other Writings of John G. Nicolay, 1860–1865* (Carbondale: Southern Illinois University Press, 2000), 89. Nicolay fretted that Iowa (which also held elections on October 14) would also "be swallowed up by the general drift." In fact, however, Republicans carried all six seats in a state that had added four seats following the 1860 census, which helped make up for the party's losses elsewhere.

14. Bruce Tap, "Race, Rhetoric, and Emancipation: The Election of 1862 in Illinois," *Civil War History* 39 (June 1993): 101, 115, 120; Jonathan Sebastian, "A Divided State: The 1862 Election and the Illinois Response to Expanding Federal Authority," *Journal of the Illinois State Historical Society* 106 (Fall-Winter 2013): 392; "Illinois State Legislature Opposes Emancipation Proclamation," January 7, 1863, in *The Civil War Archive: The History of the Civil War in Documents*, ed. Henry Steele Commanger and revised and expanded by Erik Bruun (New York: Tess Press, 2000), 613–614. The resolution also condemned the Emancipation Proclamation for inviting "servile insurrection" and thereby adopting "a means of warfare, the inhumanity and diabolism of which are without example in civilized warfare" and which constituted an "an uneffaceable disgrace to the American people."

15. Patience Essah, *A House Divided: Slavery and Emancipation in Delaware, 1838 to 1865* (Charlottesville: University of Virginia Press, 1996), 176.

16. William C. Harris, *Two against Lincoln: Reverdy Johnson and Horatio Seymour, Champions of the Loyal Opposition* (Lawrence: University Press of Kansas, 2017), 125.

17. Lincoln to Carl Schurz, November 10, 1862, in Basler, *Collected Works*, 5:494; Masur, *Lincoln's Hundred Days*, 155. For evidence that district-specific war casualties may have impacted the election, see Jamie L. Carson, Jeffery A. Jenkins, David W. Rohde, and Mark A. Souva, "The Impact of National Tides and District-Level Effects on Electoral Outcomes: The U.S. Congressional Elections of 1862–63," *American Journal of Political Science* 45 (October 2001): 887–898.

18. Lincoln to Carl Schurz, November 10, 1862, in Basler, *Collected Works*, 5:494; Tap, "Race, Rhetoric, and Emancipation," 121.

19. Tap, "Race, Rhetoric, and Emancipation," 102, 115–117, 120.

20. Tap, 109, 122, 118. Also see V. Jacque Voegeli, *Free but Not Equal: The Midwest and the Negro during the Civil War* (Chicago: University of Chicago Press, 1967), ch. 4.

21. Harris, *Two against Lincoln*, 127; Sidney David Brummer, *Political History of New York State during the Period of the Civil War* (New York: Longmans, Green, 1911), 239; also see 228–229. For turnout rates, see Walter Dean Burnham, *Voting in American Elections: The Shaping of the American Political Universe since 1788* (Palo Alto, CA: Academica Press, 2010), 338.

22. Brummer, *Political History of New York State*, 218–220, 239. On Dix's skep-

tical views of federally imposed emancipation, see V. Jacque Voegeli, "A Rejected Alternative: Union Policy and the Relocation of Southern 'Contrabands' at the Dawn of Emancipation," *Journal of Southern History* 69 (November 2003): 768.

23. Eric Foner, *The Fiery Trial: Abraham Lincoln and American Slavery* (New York: W. W. Norton, 2010), 234.

24. Those divisions within the Republican Party were on display in Illinois, where on the evening before the election the state's Republican senator Orville Browning criticized the confiscation acts, "wound up with a sneer at proclamations," and then, according to a reporter with the *Quincy Whig*, "astonished his hearers by the sage advice that they should vote for the *best ticket*, leaving it to be inferred that he did not know which was the best ticket." Sebastian, "A Divided State," 391.

25. Carson et al., "The Impact of National Tides," 887–888; Guelzo, *Lincoln's Emancipation Proclamation*, 189.

26. Guelzo, *Lincoln's Emancipation Proclamation*, 189; "Reply to Emancipation Memorial Presented by Chicago Christians of all Denominations," September 13, 1862, and Lincoln to Hamlin, September 28, 1862, in Basler, *Collected Works*, 5:423, 5:444; Voegeli, *Free but Not Equal*, 52–53.

27. James Oakes, *Freedom National: The Destruction of Slavery in the United States, 1861–1865* (New York: W. W. Norton, 2012), 330.

28. The "great mistake" quote is from a letter the abolitionist newspaper editor Theodore Tilton wrote to Wendell Phillips on Thursday, November 6, 1862, and the "minority with the people" quote is from a report later that month by Washington journalist (and Lincoln campaign biographer) D. W. Bartlett. Both are quoted in Michael Burlingame, *Abraham Lincoln: A Life* (Baltimore, MD: Johns Hopkins University Press, 2008), 2:422. On the evening before issuing the final proclamation, Lincoln reminded three abolitionist clergymen that the result of the preliminary proclamation in the fall elections was "the opposition gaining strength and carrying the majority against us. Instead of the proclamation having brought support to the administration, it has done the reverse." The abolitionists insisted that those reverses were because the proclamation postponed emancipation rather than declaring its effects immediately. Plainly unimpressed by their political naiveté, Lincoln could only shrug: "Yes, I know that is the reason you give for its failure." N. Worth Brown and Randolph C. Downes, "A Conference with Abraham Lincoln, from the diary of Reverend Nathan Brown," *Northwest Ohio Quarterly* 22 (1950): 58–59, https://toledosattic.org/images/pdfs/nwoq-by-issue/NWOQ_1950_Vol22-2.pdf.

29. On the concept of "professional reputation," see Richard E. Neustadt, *Presidential Power: The Politics of Leadership* (New York: Wiley, 1960), ch. 4.

CHAPTER 7. ON DEAF EARS

1. Gillian Brockell, "Where Did All the Strange State of the Union Traditions Come From?," *Washington Post*, February 7, 2023, https://www.washingtonpost.com/history/2023/02/07/state-of-the-union-traditions-origins/.

2. *Baltimore Sun*, December 2, 1862, 4.

3. David Davis to Leonard Swett, November 26, 1862, quoted in David Herbert Donald, *Lincoln* (New York: Simon & Schuster, 1995), 397; "Preliminary Emancipation Proclamation," September 22, 1861, in Roy P. Basler, ed., *The Collected Works of Abraham Lincoln* (New Brunswick, NJ: Rutgers University Press, 1953), 5:434

4. "Annual Message to Congress," December 1, 1862, in Basler, *Collected Works*, 5:536. Charles Sumner's "olive branch" quote can be found in Michael Burlingame, *Abraham Lincoln: A Life* (Baltimore, MD: Johns Hopkins University Press, 2008), 2:441. Lincoln's calculation that approval of an amendment would require the assent of seven slave states reflected the fact that the United States at this time was made up of fifteen slave states (four that never left the Union and eleven that joined the Confederacy) and twenty free states. The three-fourths threshold could only be reached if twenty-seven states backed an amendment.

5. "Annual Message to Congress," in Basler, *Collected Works*, 5:530.

6. "Annual Message to Congress," 5:530–531.

7. "Annual Message to Congress," 5:531–532.

8. "Annual Message to Congress," 5:532–534.

9. "Annual Message to Congress," 5:534.

10. "Annual Message to Congress," 5:535.

11. "Annual Message to Congress," 5:535–536. Some northern states, including Lincoln's own state of Illinois as well as Indiana and Oregon, already had provisions in their state constitutions that forbid Blacks from entering the state. Mark E. Neely Jr., *Lincoln and the Triumph of the Nation: Constitutional Conflict in the American Civil War* (Chapel Hill: University of North Carolina Press, 2011), 114–115. In addition to offering tacit approval of what Neely calls "constitutional racism," Lincoln lent legitimacy to the popular idea of "isothermalism," which reassured Whites in the North that freed slaves would remain in "congenial climes" in the South. Mark E. Neely Jr., "Colonization and the Myth that Lincoln Prepared the People for Emancipation," in *Lincoln's Proclamation: Emancipation Reconsidered*, ed. William A. Blair and Karen Fisher Younger (Chapel Hill: University of North Carolina Press, 2009), 64–65.

12. "Annual Message to Congress," in Basler, *Collected Works*, 5:535–537.

13. "Annual Message to Congress," 5:537; Allen C. Guelzo, *Lincoln's Emancipation Proclamation: The End of Slavery in America* (New York: Simon & Schuster, 2004), 196; Burlingame, *Abraham Lincoln*, 2:442.

14. Guelzo, *Lincoln's Emancipation Proclamation*, 196; Eric Foner, *The Fiery Trial: Abraham Lincoln and American Slavery* (New York: W. W. Norton, 2010), 238; diary entry, December 1, 1862, in Theodore Calvin Pease and James G. Randall, eds., *The Diary of Orville Hickman Browning* (Springfield: Illinois State Historical Library, 1925), 1:591; Louis Masur, *Lincoln's Hundred Days: The Emancipation Proclamation and the War for the Union* (Cambridge, MA: Harvard University Press, 2012), 180; Burlingame, *Abraham Lincoln*, 2:440.

15. Foner, *The Fiery Trial*, 238.

16. Burlingame, *Abraham Lincoln*, 2:442. Lincoln did succeed in winning some important converts in Missouri, including US senator John Henderson and the state's governor, Hamilton Gamble, both of whom had come around to the view that the war was fast making the abolition of slavery all but inevitable, so that Missouri should seek federal compensation while they still could. William Harris, *Lincoln and the Border States: Preserving the Union* (Lawrence: University Press of Kansas, 2011), 205-206. On December 10, 1862, Henderson introduced a bill, which Lincoln may have drafted (Burlingame, *Abraham Lincoln*, 2:443), that would appropriate federal funds to compensate Missouri's slaveowners. Lincoln regarded the legislation as vital to the Union's success, telling New Hampshire senator John Hale in early January that "you and I must die but it will be enough for us to have done in our lives if we make Missouri free" (Pease and Randall, *Diary of Orville Hickman Browning*, 1:612). Although the Senate passed an amended version of the bill in February, Henderson was the only border state senator to back it, and opponents of the legislation in the House managed to prevent the bill from coming to a vote (Harris, *Lincoln and the Border States*, 220-221), a defeat that left Lincoln "bitterly disappointed." Burlingame, *Abraham Lincoln*, 2:443.

17. David Davis to Leonard Swett, November 26, 1862, quoted in Burlingame, *Abraham Lincoln*, 2:442.

18. Burlingame, *Abraham Lincoln*, 2:439.

19. Guelzo, *Lincoln's Emancipation Proclamation*, 193-194; Noah Feldman, *The Broken Constitution: Lincoln, Slavery, and the Refounding of America* (New York: Farrar, Straus & Giroux, 2021), 294.

20. Burlingame, *Abraham Lincoln*, 2:442.

21. Charles Sumner to Wendell Phillips, December 4, 1862, in Beverly Wilson Palmer, ed., *The Selected Letters of Charles Sumner* (Boston: Northeastern University Press, 1990), 2:133.

22. Sumner to Wendell Phillips, December 4, 1862, in Palmer, *The Selected Letters of Charles Sumner*, 2:133; Burlingame, *Abraham Lincoln*, 2:441; Masur, *Lincoln's Hundred Days*, 183. Also see James N. McPherson, *The Struggle for Equality: Abolitionists and the Negro in the Civil War* (Princeton, NJ: Princeton University Press, 1964), 120.

23. "Annual Message to Congress," in Basler, *Collected Works*, 5:530; Burlingame, *Abraham Lincoln*, 2:440. In assuring Wendell Phillips of Lincoln's intentions to emancipate the slaves, Sumner said, "The last paragraph of the message is everything. All the rest is surplusage." Sumner to Phillips, December 4, 1862, in Palmer, *The Selected Letters of Charles Sumner*, 2:133.

CHAPTER 8. "AN ACT OF JUSTICE"

1. James N. McPherson, *The Struggle for Equality: Abolitionists and the Negro in the Civil War* (Princeton, NJ: Princeton University Press, 1964), 120. The question was posed by Moncure Conway, an abolitionist with the unusual distinction of

having been born into a prominent Virginia slaveholding family and having two brothers serving in the Confederate army.

2. Mark E. Neely Jr., *Lincoln and the Triumph of the Nation: Constitutional Conflict in the American Civil War* (Chapel Hill: University of North Carolina Press, 2011), 131; "Remarks to Union Kentuckians," November 21, 1862, in Roy P. Basler, ed., *The Collected Works of Abraham Lincoln* (New Brunswick, NJ: Rutgers University Press, 1953), 5:503. These remarks were according to a report appearing in Greeley's *New York Tribune* on November 24, 1862. On Lincoln's determination not to revoke the Emancipation Proclamation, a proposition he reportedly described as "preposterous," see the exchange related in Louis Masur, *Lincoln's Hundred Days: The Emancipation Proclamation and the War for the Union* (Cambridge, MA: Harvard University Press, 2012), 167–168.

3. Charles Sumner to John Murray Forbes, December 28, 1862, in Beverly Wilson Palmer, ed., *The Selected Letters of Charles Sumner* (Boston: Northeastern University Press, 1990), 2:136. Sumner reported Lincoln's words the same way in a letter that same day to Samuel Gridley Howe, who in March 1863 would be appointed to the three-person American Freedmen's Inquiry Commission. McPherson, *The Struggle for Equality*, 120.

4. Diary entry, December 31, 1862, in Theodore Calvin Pease and James G. Randall, eds., *The Diary of Orville Hickman Browning* (Springfield: Illinois State Historical Library, 1925), 1:607.

5. Michael Burlingame, *Abraham Lincoln: A Life* (Baltimore, MD: Johns Hopkins University Press, 2008), 2:439, 448–449; Masur, *Lincoln's Hundred Days*, 187. On the final day of December, William Dickson (a Lincoln elector from Ohio in 1860 whose wife was a cousin of Mary Todd Lincoln) wrote to a friend, the US minister to Ecuador, to report that he had spoken with a broad range of members of Congress and military officers and they were "united in ascribing to the President the honor of being the author of all our calamities. His imbecility, vacillation, meddling interference with everything, his frivolity and total incapacity of receiving or appreciating [advice] make him the most incorrigible stumbling block that God ever afflicted any nation with." Burlingame, *Abraham Lincoln*, 2:448.

6. Burlingame, 2:449–451.

7. Burlingame, 2:453; Pease and Randall, *Diary of Orville Hickman Browning*, 1:600–601.

8. Burlingame, *Abraham Lincoln*, 2:450–451, 457; Masur, *Lincoln's Hundred Days*, 186.

9. The "stand firm" language was used by Harriet Beecher Stowe in a letter to Charles Sumner on December 12 and George Templeton Strong in a diary entry of December 27. Strong added that if Lincoln postponed or diluted the proclamation, "his name will be a byword and a hissing till the annals of the nineteenth century are forgotten." Masur, *Lincoln's Hundred Days*, 191.

10. In the November meeting with Kentucky Unionists, congressman Samuel Casey told Lincoln that while he initially opposed the proclamation he would

not "desire him to do so cowardly a thing as retrace your steps at the dictation of Democrats and slaveholders." Masur, *Lincoln's Hundred Days*, 198.

11. David Donald, *Lincoln* (New York: Simon & Schuster, 1995), 423.

12. "The Proclamation of Freedom," *New York Tribune*, December 30, 1862, 5; the short report is from a special dispatch to the *Tribune* from Washington and is dated December 29, 1862. It is printed in full in Masur, *Lincoln's Hundred Days*, 200.

13. John Murray Forbes to Charles Sumner, December 27, 1862, in Sarah Forbes Hughes, ed., *Letters and Recollections of John Murray Forbes*, 2 vols. (Boston: Houghton, Mifflin, 1900), 1:350–351, emphasis in original. In his letter to Sumner, Forbes enclosed a petition signed by all but one of Lincoln's electors in 1860 that urged the president to "complete now your great work" by issuing the proclamation. Sumner presented the petition to the president that evening. Masur, *Lincoln's Hundred Days*, 193.

14. Charles Sumner to John Murray Forbes, December 28, 1862, in Hughes, *Letters and Recollections of John Murray Forbes*, 1:352. The *Selected Letters of Sumner* mistakenly renders "benevolent God" as "benevolent Govt" (2:136). "The Proclamation of Freedom," *New York Tribune*, December 30, 1862, 5.

15. Burlingame, *Abraham Lincoln*, 2:463; diary entry of December 31, 1862, in William E. Gienapp and Erica L. Gienapp, eds., *Civil War Diary of Gideon Welles, Lincoln's Secretary of the Navy* (Urbana: University of Illinois Press, 2014), 111; John Hope Franklin, *The Emancipation Proclamation* (Wheeling, IL: Harlan Davidson, 1995; first published 1963), 76–77. Chase not only proposed significant revisions to the proclamation but drafted a separate memorandum that was essentially an entirely new proclamation that recounted some of the many steps Lincoln had taken to avoid interfering with slavery and indicted the South for having remained "obstinately deaf" to Lincoln's eminently reasonable appeals and proposals, leaving the administration no other recourse than emancipation. Salmon P. Chase, Memorandum in Emancipation, [December 31?, 1862], Abraham Lincoln Papers, Series 1, General Correspondence, 1833–1916, Library of Congress, http://www.loc.gov/resource/mal.2083500, hereafter cited as ALP.

16. In a letter to George Livermore, dated January 9, 1863, Sumner reported that while the final sentence was framed by Chase, he was the first to urge the president to close with "something about justice & God." Sumner said that he suggested a sentence that closed by declaring the proclamation not only an act of military necessity but "also an act of justice to an oppressed race, which must draw down upon our country the favor of a beneficent God." Palmer, *Selected Letters*, 2:140. Also see Burrus M. Carnahan, *Act of Justice: Lincoln's Emancipation Proclamation and the Law of War* (Lexington: University Press of Kentucky, 2007), esp. 115.

17. Forbes to Sumner, December 27, 1862, in Hughes, *Letters and Recollections of John Murray Forbes*, 350.

18. Burlingame, *Abraham Lincoln*, 2:464. Section 11 of the Second Confiscation Act provided an even more broadly worded authorization: "That the President of the United States is authorized to employ as many persons of African descent

as he may deem necessary and proper for the suppression of this rebellion, and for this purpose he may organize and use them in such manner as he may judge best for the public welfare." The full text of the act can be found at "Second Confiscation Act: 'Chap. CXCV—An Act to Suppress Insurrection, to Punish Treason and Rebellion . . . ,' July 17, 1862," State Historical Society of Iowa, accessed July 19, 2024, https://history.iowa.gov/history/education/educator-resources/primary-source-sets/african-americans-and-civil-war/second.

19. Burlingame, *Abraham Lincoln*, 2:465; James Oakes, *Freedom National: The Destruction of Slavery in the United States, 1861–1865* (New York: W. W. Norton, 2012), 377.

20. Oakes, *Freedom National*, 378; Burlingame, *Abraham Lincoln*, 2:465; Lincoln, "Preliminary Draft of Final Emancipation Proclamation" [December 30, 1862], in Basler, *Collected Works*, 6:24.

21. Edward Bates, "Memorandum on the Emancipation Proclamation," December 31, 1862, ALP, http://www.loc.gov/resource/mal.2081800; Salmon P. Chase to Abraham Lincoln, December 31, 1862 (Recommended alterations to the Emancipation Proclamation), ALP, http://www.loc.gov/resource/mal.2063900.

22. Chase to Abraham Lincoln, Wednesday, December 31, 1862, ALP; Lincoln, "Preliminary Draft of Final Emancipation Proclamation," in Basler, *Collected Works*, 6:24; William H. Seward to Abraham Lincoln, December 30, 1862, ALP, http://www.loc.gov/resource/mal.2059600. In the final draft of the proclamation, Lincoln dropped "disorder" and "tumult," leaving only the appeal to avoid violence. Instead of Lincoln's appeal, Chase preferred "not . . . encouraging or in any way sanctioning any disorderly conduct or licentious violence." Salmon P. Chase, "Proposed Revision of Emancipation Proclamation," [December 30–31?, 1862], ALP, http://www.loc.gov/resource/mal.2083000.

23. Chase, "Proposed Revision," ALP; Seward to Lincoln, December 30, 1862, ALP. Although Lincoln dropped the clause in the final proclamation, the proclamation began by quoting verbatim the third and fourth paragraphs of the preliminary proclamation, which included the original "do no act" language.

24. Oakes, *Freedom National*, 367.

25. Oakes, ch. 6.

26. Oakes, 368; Washington Correspondence, September 22, 1862, in Michael Burlingame, ed., *Lincoln's Journalist: John Hay's Anonymous Writings for the Press, 1860–1864* (Carbondale: Southern Illinois University Press, 1998), 309.

27. Masur, *Lincoln's Hundred Days*, 197.

28. Eric Foner, *The Fiery Trial: Abraham Lincoln and American Slavery* (New York: W. W. Norton, 2010), 239–240, 259–260. Also see Philip W. Magness and Sebastian N. Page, *Colonization after Emancipation: Lincoln and the Movement for Black Resettlement* (Columbia: University of Missouri Press, 2011).

29. Oakes, *Freedom National*, 362. Lincoln qualified the requirement by noting that congressional elections would be "deemed conclusive evidence . . . in the absence of strong countervailing testimony." Preliminary Emancipation Proclamation, September 22, 1862, in Basler, *Collected Works*, 5:434.

30. Chase to Lincoln, Wednesday, December 31, 1862, ALP; Foner, *Fiery Trial*, 238–239. Welles backed Chase's objection to exempting parts of states. Diary entry of December 29, 1862, in Gienapp and Gienapp, *Civil War Diary of Gideon Welles*, 110.

31. Foner, *Fiery Trial*, 243, 239.

32. Foner, 243.

33. Foner, 238; Chase to Lincoln, December 31, 1862, ALP; Masur, *Lincoln's Hundred Days*, 189.

34. Masur, *Lincoln's Hundred Days*, 189–190.

35. Lincoln, "Opinion on the Admission of West Virginia into the Union," in Basler, *Collected Works*, 6:27–28; Masur, *Lincoln's Hundred Days*, 190; Allen C. Guelzo, *Lincoln's Emancipation Proclamation: The End of Slavery in America* (New York: Simon & Schuster, 2004), 200.

36. Frederick W. Seward, *Reminiscences of a War-time Statesman and Diplomat, 1830–1915* (New York: G. P. Putnam's Sons, 1916), 227; Guelzo, *Lincoln's Emancipation Proclamation*, 205–206; Burlingame, *Abraham Lincoln* 2:469.

37. On the evening of December 31, 1862, Lincoln met with a delegation of three abolitionist ministers who urged "upon the President the duty of carrying out emancipation as a measure of *justice*; and not as a mere military necessity." Lincoln responded that he "considered that he had no power to do it except as a military measure," and while "he would be glad to have slavery done away with, . . . he knew no authority by which he could interfere, except as a measure of war." N. Worth Brown and Randolph C. Downes, "A Conference with Abraham Lincoln, from the diary of Reverend Nathan Brown," *Northwest Ohio Quarterly* 22 (1950): 61, https://toledosattic.org/images/pdfs/nwoq-by-issue/NWOQ_1950_Vol22-2.pdf.

38. Andrew Rudalevige, *By Executive Order: Bureaucratic Management and the Limits of Presidential Power* (Princeton, NJ: Princeton University Press, 2021), x.

CHAPTER 9. A LESS THAN CONCLUSIVE ORDER

1. Jessica Tyler Austen, ed., *Moses Coit Tyler, 1835–1900: Selections from His Letters and Diaries* (Garden City, NY: Doubleday, Page, 1911), 17–19 (December 18, 22, 1862, January 1, 1863); Michael Kammen, "Moses Coit Tyler: The First Professor of American History in the United States," *History Teacher* 17 (Nov. 1983): 61–87; Louis Masur, *The Emancipation Proclamation and the War for the Union* (Cambridge, MA: Harvard University Press, 2012), 205. Garrison, who Coit had visited just a few days before, made the same comparison with July Fourth in the pages of the *Liberator*. "The first day of January, 1863," Garrison proclaimed, "has now taken rank with the fourth of July, 1776, in the history of this country. The Proclamation, though leaving much to be done in the future, clears our course from all doubt and our process from all uncertainty." John Hope Franklin, *The Emancipation Proclamation* (Wheeling, IL: Harlan Davidson, 1995; first published 1963), 91.

2. Eric Foner, *The Fiery Trial: Abraham Lincoln and American Slavery* (New York: W. W. Norton, 2010), 247, emphasis added.

3. Richard Hofstadter, *The American Political Tradition and the Men Who Made It* (New York: Vintage Books, 1974), 169.

4. Masur, *The Emancipation Proclamation*, 216–217.

5. Frances Carpenter, *The Inner Life of Abraham Lincoln: Six Months at the White House* (Lincoln: University of Nebraska Press, 1985), 90; N. Worth Brown and Randolph C. Downes, "A Conference with Abraham Lincoln, from the diary of Reverend Nathan Brown," *Northwest Ohio Quarterly* 22 (1950): 56, 60–61, https://toledosattic.org/images/pdfs/nwoq-by-issue/NWOQ_1950_Vol22-2.pdf. Similarly, in a meeting at the White House on January 25, 1863, when the abolitionist Wendell Phillips asked Lincoln how he felt the proclamation was working, he replied that "he had not expected much from it at first, and so had not been disappointed." But while adding that "at no time" had he "expected any sudden results from" the proclamation, he nonetheless believed it "has knocked the bottom out of slavery." Moncure Daniel Conway, *Autobiography, Memories and Experience* (London: Cassell, 1904), 1:336, 338.

6. Brown and Downes, "A Conference with Abraham Lincoln," 61–62.

7. Richard E. Neustadt, *Presidential Power: The Politics of Leadership* (New York: Wiley, 1960), 10, 29–30.

8. "Reply to Emancipation Memorial Presented by Chicago Christians of all Denominations," September 13, 1862, in Roy P. Basler, ed., *The Collected Works of Abraham Lincoln* (New Brunswick, NJ: Rutgers University Press, 1953), 5:420.

9. Masur, *Lincoln's Hundred Days*, 212–213. On Lincoln's Cooper Union speech, which he delivered on February 27, 1860, see Harold Holzer, *Lincoln at Cooper Union: The Speech that Made Abraham Lincoln President* (New York: Simon & Schuster, 2004).

10. Jonathan W. White, *Emancipation, the Union Army, and the Reelection of Abraham Lincoln* (Baton Rouge: Louisiana State University Press, 2014), 9, 154, 81, 85, 40, 19, 76. Lincoln recognized the problem, which he alluded to obliquely in a letter to one of his generals in which he proposed using "colored troops" to garrison two forts, thereby enabling "white forces . . . to be employed elsewhere." Lincoln explained that "we were not succeeding—at best, were progressing too slowly—without [the proclamation]. Now, that we have it, and bear all the disadvantage of it, (as we do bear some in certain quarters) we must also take some benefit from it, if practicable." Lincoln to John A. Dix, January 14, 1863, in Basler, *Collected Works*, 6:56.

11. Oakes, *Freedom National*, 371–372; White, *Emancipation, the Union Army, and the Reelection of Abraham Lincoln*, 39–40.

12. White, *Emancipation, the Union Army, and the Reelection of Abraham Lincoln*, 39, 91, 40.

13. White, 95–96.

14. Oakes, *Freedom National*, 418; "Camp Nelson National Cemetery," National Park Service, accessed June 9, 2024, https://www.nps.gov/nr/travel/national_cemeteries/kentucky/camp_nelson_national_cemetery.html. The expulsion order was issued on November 23, 1864, and countermanded on November 29, 1864.

15. Phineas Camp Headley, *The Life and Campaigns of General U.S. Grant* (New York: Geo. A. Leavitt, 1869), 217–218; Oakes, *Freedom National*, 368–369.

16. Oakes, *Freedom National*, 370, 372.

17. Oakes, 373, 344.

18. In the final version of the proclamation—and without explanation—Lincoln dropped the phrase "forever free." The "forever free" language was used in the Second Confiscation Act, and Lincoln adopted it in the preliminary proclamation. The phrase was also in the draft of the final proclamation that the cabinet discussed at the end of December. Why Lincoln made this last-minute change "remains unknown" (Foner, *Fiery Trial*, 239), but Allen Guelzo speculates that Lincoln may have altered the wording because "he had never believed that a military proclamation could guarantee freedom *forever*, beyond the time of the war emergency that called for it," and so "rather than give the judges even one spike to hang the Proclamation on, . . . [he] withdrew what he knew he could not actually promise." Allen C. Guelzo, *Lincoln's Emancipation Proclamation: The End of Slavery in America* (New York: Simon & Schuster, 2004), 204. Michael Burlingame also ventures that Lincoln may have dropped "forever" because he "feared that the courts would take a dim view of such an extravagant claim." Michael Burlingame, *Abraham Lincoln: A Life* (Baltimore, MD: Johns Hopkins University Press, 2008), 2:463.

19. Oakes, *Freedom National*, 395; David Herbert Donald, *Lincoln* (New York: Simon & Schuster, 1995), 455.

20. Oakes, *Freedom National*, 345; Lincoln to James C. Conkling, August 26, 1863, in Basler, *Collected Works*, 6:406; Donald, *Lincoln*, 456; Guelzo, *Lincoln's Emancipation Proclamation*, 236.

21. Lincoln to Conkling, in Basler, *Collected Works*, 6:407.

22. Lincoln to Conkling, 6:408. Lincoln's principal goal was to defend the Emancipation Proclamation, but he could not resist a dig at those who had balked at his favored plan of compensated emancipation: "I suggested compensated emancipation, to which you replied you wished not to be taxed to buy negroes. But I had not asked you to be taxed to buy negroes, except in such way as to save you from greater taxation to save the Union exclusively by other means" (6:407–408).

23. Lincoln to Conkling, 6:408–409.

24. Lincoln to Conkling, 6:409.

25. Lincoln to Conkling, 6:409.

26. Lincoln to Conkling, 6:409–410, emphasis added. Lincoln's spirits were buoyed too by the success of the Unionists in elections held in Kentucky in early August.

27. Guelzo, *Lincoln's Emancipation Proclamation*, 239; Burlingame, *Abraham Lincoln*, 2:562.

28. Donald, *Lincoln*, 456; Guelzo, *Lincoln's Emancipation Proclamation*, 235.

29. Donald, *Lincoln*, 458. Continuing abolitionist discontent with the "half-converted" Lincoln (Burlingame, *Abraham Lincoln*, 2:637) led many abolitionists to

flirt with the third-party challenge of the Radical Democracy Party, which at the end of May 1864 nominated General John Frémont for the presidency. Frémont would eventually withdraw from the race in the latter part of September.

30. Burlingame, *Abraham Lincoln*, 2:667, 658. In mid-August, for instance, Weed told Lincoln that his reelection "was an impossibility" (2:668; Basler, *Collected Works*, 7:514), and Leonard Swett judged that without a dramatic change in the trajectory of the war, reelection was "beyond any possible hope" (Burlingame, *Abraham Lincoln*, 2:668).

31. Burlingame, *Abraham Lincoln*, 2:668-669. On the attempts to dump Lincoln, see 2:665-667. Those fears had been stoked by the leak of the so-called Niagara Manifesto (so-called by Democrats), in which Lincoln specified that the preconditions for any peace negotiations included not only the restoration of the Union but "the abandonment of slavery." On the politics of this episode, see Burlingame, *Abraham Lincoln*, 2:669-672.

32. "Memorandum Concerning His Probable Failure of Re-election," August 23, 1864, in Basler, *Collected Works*, 7:514; Oakes, *Freedom National*, 472-473, 405; Burlingame, *Abraham Lincoln*, 2:677.

33. Oakes, *Freedom National*, 371, 474; Burlingame, *Abraham Lincoln*, 2:677.

34. Oakes, *Freedom National*, 474; Burlingame, *Abraham Lincoln*, 2:677; James Oakes, *The Radical and the Republican: Frederick Douglass, Abraham Lincoln, and the Triumph of Antislavery Politics* (New York: W. W. Norton, 2007), 225, 232.

35. Conway, *Autobiography*, 1:339. Also see Burlingame, *Abraham Lincoln*, 2:677.

36. Oakes, *Freedom National*, 416-417, 419; also see 222.

37. Oakes, 421-422; Oakes, *The Radical and the Republican*, 230.

38. Oakes, *Freedom National*, 396, 421.

39. Oakes, 381.

40. Oakes, 427, 397.

CONCLUSION: LESSONS AND LEGACIES

1. Richard Hofstadter, *The American Political Tradition and the Men Who Made It* (New York: Vintage Books, 1974), 169-170; Lerone Bennett Jr., *Forced into Glory: Abraham Lincoln's White Dream* (Chicago: Johnson Publishing, 2007).

2. Allen C. Guelzo, *Lincoln's Emancipation Proclamation: The End of Slavery in America* (New York: Simon & Schuster, 2004), 30.

3. Richard E. Neustadt, *Presidential Power and the Modern Presidents: The Politics of Leadership from Roosevelt to Reagan* (New York: Free Press, 1990), xix.

4. Washington Correspondence, September 22, 1862, in Michael Burlingame, ed., *Lincoln's Journalist: John Hay's Anonymous Writings for the Press, 1860-1864* (Carbondale: Southern Illinois University Press, 1998), 309.

5. James Oakes, *Freedom National: The Destruction of Slavery in the United States, 1861-1865* (New York: W. W. Norton, 2012), 362.

6. Oakes, 360.

7. Dino P. Christenson and Douglas L. Kriner, *The Myth of the Imperial Presi-*

dency: How Public Opinion Checks the Unilateral Executive (Chicago: University of Chicago Press, 2020), 25.

8. Ronald C. White, *The Eloquent President: A Portrait of Lincoln Through His Words* (New York: Random House, 2003).

9. Louis Masur, *Lincoln's Hundred Days: The Emancipation Proclamation and the War for the Union* (Cambridge, MA: Harvard University Press, 2012), 211.

10. Oakes, *Freedom National*, 367.

11. William Harris, *Lincoln and the Border States: Preserving the Union* (University Press of Kansas, 2011), 282, 295, 300. In Maryland, a division among those seeking gradual and immediate emancipation threatened to derail the effort to abolish slavery, which impelled Lincoln to clarify his position. "My expressions of a preference for *gradual* over *immediate* emancipation are misunderstood," he told Maryland representative John Creswell. "I had thought the *gradual* would produce less confusion, and destitution, and therefore would be more satisfactory; but if those who are better acquainted with the subject, and more deeply interested in it, prefer the *immediate*, most certainly I have no objection to their judgment prevailing." What mattered to Lincoln was the achievement of "emancipation *in any form*." Lincoln to John A. J. Creswell, March 7, 1864, in Roy P. Basler, ed., *The Collected Works of Abraham Lincoln* (New Brunswick, NJ: Rutgers University Press, 1953), 7:226.

12. Neustadt, *Presidential Power*, 29.

13. Eric Foner, *The Fiery Trial: Abraham Lincoln and American Slavery* (New York: W. W. Norton, 2010), 243.

14. Oakes, *Freedom National*, 428.

15. Foner, *The Fiery Trial*, 244.

16. Oakes, *Freedom National*.

17. Oakes, 335; Ira Berlin, "Who Freed the Slaves? Emancipation and Its Meaning?" in *Union and Emancipation: Essays on Politics and Race in the Civil War Era*, edited by David W. Blight and Brooks D. Simpson (Kent, OH: Kent State University Press, 1997), 209n37. "The Master Politician" is a chapter title in Richard N. Current, *The Lincoln Nobody Knows* (New York: McGraw-Hill, 1956), 187–213.

18. Foner, *The Fiery Trial*, 246; Mark E. Neely Jr., *Lincoln and the Triumph of the Nation: Constitutional Conflict in the American Civil War* (Chapel Hill: University of North Carolina Press, 2011), 128.

19. Charles Sumner to Francis Lieber, September 17, 1861, in Beverly Wilson Palmer, ed., *The Selected Letters of Charles Sumner* (Boston: Northeastern University Press, 1990), 2:79.

20. Oakes, *Freedom National*, 335.

BIBLIOGRAPHIC ESSAY

"Has the Lincoln Theme Been Exhausted?" That was the question historian James G. Randall posed almost a century ago. Judging by the unrelenting torrent of work on Lincoln, the answer seems to be a resounding "no." There is, by far, more written about Lincoln than any other person in American history. Indeed, according to one count, now more than a decade old, something in the order of fifteen thousand books have been penned about Lincoln, which is reputedly more than has been written about anybody in world history except Jesus Christ. With that immense quantity, however, has come remarkable quality. What follows below is necessarily a highly selective accounting of the Lincoln literature that is relevant to the Emancipation Proclamation. I have limited myself to books to make the task more manageable, although the reader will find journal articles that I have relied on cited in the endnotes.

The obvious starting place for students interested in reading a fuller account of the Emancipation Proclamation is Louis Masur, *Lincoln's Hundred Days: The Emancipation Proclamation and the War for the Union* (Cambridge, MA: Harvard University Press, 2012), and Allen C. Guelzo, *Lincoln's Emancipation Proclamation: The End of Slavery in America* (New York: Simon & Schuster, 2004). Still valuable is the admirably concise volume by John Hope Franklin, *The Emancipation Proclamation* (Wheeling, IL: Harlan Davidson, 1995; first published in 1963), written to commemorate the centennial of the signing of the Emancipation Proclamation. Although neither Lincoln nor the Emancipation Proclamation appear in its title, James Oakes, *Freedom National: The Destruction of Slavery in the United States, 1861–1865* (New York: W. W. Norton, 2012) is indispensable in understanding the Proclamation's place in the destruction of slavery in the United States. Equally indispensable in thinking about Lincoln's relationship to slavery is Eric Foner, *The Fiery Trial: Abraham Lincoln and American Slavery* (New York: W. W. Norton, 2010). A concise treatment is offered in Edna Greene Medford, *Lincoln and Emancipation* (Carbondale: Southern Illinois University Press, 2015), one of the thirty (and counting) volumes published as part of the Concise Lincoln Library that covers all manner of Lincoln-related topics (http://siupress.siu.edu/series/concise-lincoln-library). Also see William K. Klingaman, *Abraham Lincoln and the Road to Emancipation, 1861–1865* (New York: Penguin, 2002), and Benjamin Quarles, *Lincoln and the Negro* (New York: Oxford University Press, 1962).

Other valuable books focused on the Proclamation specifically are Harold Holzer, *Emancipating Lincoln: The Proclamation in Text, Context, and Memory* (Cambridge, MA: Harvard University Press, 2012); Burrus M. Carnahan, *Act of Justice: Lincoln's Emancipation Proclamation and the Law of War* (Lexington: University Press of Kentucky, 2007); Harold Holzer, Edna Greene Medford, and Frank J. Williams, *The Emancipation Proclamation* (Baton Rouge: Louisiana State University Press, 2006); and William A. Blair and Karen Fisher Younger, eds., *Lincoln's Proclamation: Emancipation Reconsidered* (Chapel Hill: University of North Carolina Press, 2009), a rich volume that includes among its many fine chapters a provocative essay by Mark E. Neely Jr., "Colonization and the Myth that Lincoln Prepared the People for Emancipation." Neely's argument is powerfully amplified in Mark E. Neely Jr., *Lincoln and the Triumph of the Nation: Constitutional Conflict in the American Civil War* (Chapel Hill: University of North Carolina Press, 2011), particularly in chapter 3 ("The Emancipation Proclamation: The Triumph of Nationalism over Racism and the Constitution"). Geared to classroom use is the wide-ranging collection of primary documents in Michael Vorenberg, ed., *The Emancipation Proclamation: A Brief History with Documents* (New York: Bedford/St. Martin's, 2010), which also includes a valuable introductory essay by the editor and closes with two sharply contrasting but equally illuminating assessments of the question of "who freed the slaves?" by James M. McPherson and Ira Berlin. McPherson's essay is excerpted from an essay of that title in his collection of essays, *Drawn with the Sword: Reflections on the American Civil War* (New York: Oxford University Press, 1996). Berlin's essay is taken from his chapter "Who Freed the Slaves? Emancipation and Its Meaning," in *Union and Emancipation: Essays on Politics and Race in the Civil War Era*, ed. David W. Blight and Brooks D. Simpson (Kent, OH: Kent State University Press, 1997). Also see Barbara Jeanne Fields, "Who Freed the Slaves?" in *The Civil War: An Illustrated History*, ed. Geoffrey Ward (New York: Knopf, 1990), and

Vincent Harding, *There Is a River: The Black Struggle for Freedom in America* (New York: Houghton Mifflin, 1981).

Other, more specialized studies that I found particularly useful in thinking about the Emancipation Proclamation include William Harris, *Lincoln and the Border States: Preserving the Union* (Lawrence: University Press of Kansas, 2011); Jonathan W. White, *Emancipation, the Union Army, and the Reelection of Abraham Lincoln* (Baton Rouge: Louisiana State University Press, 2014); and Douglas L. Wilson, *Lincoln's Sword: The Presidency and the Power of Words* (New York: Vintage, 2006). Recent books that are useful in exploring Lincoln's thinking about slavery include James Oakes, *The Crooked Path to Abolition: Abraham Lincoln and the Antislavery Constitution* (New York: W. W. Norton, 2021); Michael Burlingame, *The Black Man's President: Abraham Lincoln, African Americans, and the Pursuit of Racial Equality* (New York: Pegasus, 2021); Noah Feldman, *The Broken Constitution: Lincoln, Slavery, and the Refounding of America* (New York: Farrar, Straus & Giroux, 2021); and James H. Read, *Sovereign of a Free People: Abraham Lincoln, Majority Rule, and Slavery* (Lawrence: University Press of Kansas, 2023), which, without in any way minimizing the centrality of slavery, highlights Lincoln's overarching commitment to peaceful, democratic processes—what Lincoln in his July 4, 1861, message to Congress described as "time, discussion, and the ballot box"—in resolving the sectional conflict. Other books, with a range of perspectives on Lincoln, race, and slavery, include LaWanda Cox, *Lincoln and Black Freedom: A Study in Presidential Leadership* (Columbia: University of South Carolina Press, 1981); David E. Long, *The Jewel of Liberty: Abraham Lincoln's Reelection and the End of Slavery* (Mechanicsburg, PA: Stackpole Books, 1994); Lerone Bennett Jr., *Forced into Glory: Abraham Lincoln's White Dream* (Chicago: Johnson Publishing, 2000); Richard Striner, *Father Abraham: Lincoln's Relentless Struggle to End Slavery* (New York: Oxford University Press, 2007); Brian R. Dirck, *Abraham Lincoln and White America* (Lawrence: University Press of Kansas, 2012); and Daniel Crofts, *Lincoln and the Politics of Slavery: The Other Thirteenth Amendment and the Struggle to Save the Union* (Chapel Hill: University of North Carolina Press, 2016). Not focused on Lincoln but essential to understanding the situation Lincoln faced in dealing with slavery is V. Jacque Voegeli, *Free but Not Equal: The Midwest and the*

Negro during the Civil War (Chicago: University of Chicago Press, 1967). Also see Harold Holzer, *Lincoln and the Power of the Press: The War for Public Opinion* (New York: Simon & Schuster, 2014).

Precisely because the Emancipation Proclamation was a "landmark presidential decision," it figures prominently in virtually any Lincoln biography and certainly any account of the Lincoln presidency. And, of course, the number of Lincoln biographies are legion, and the excellence of many of them means that the reader is spoiled for choice. The most comprehensive by far is Michael Burlingame's two-volume *Abraham Lincoln: A Life* (Baltimore, MD: Johns Hopkins University Press, 2008). For those daunted by its two thousand pages, there is now an abridged version of Burlingame's master work that condenses it into a single volume of closer to seven hundred pages; it is abridged and edited by Jonathan W. White and was published in 2023 by Johns Hopkins University Press. Another monumental achievement in Lincoln biography is *The Political Life of Abraham Lincoln* by Sidney Blumenthal, which so far counts three volumes: *A Self-Made Man, 1809–1849* (New York: Simon & Schuster, 2016); *Wrestling with His Angel, 1849–1856* (New York: Simon & Schuster, 2017); and *All the Powers of Earth, 1856–1860* (New York: Simon & Schuster, 2019). The planned final two volumes will cover his presidential years. Among other recent, highly readable biographies are David S. Reynolds, *Abe: Abraham Lincoln in His Times* (New York: Penguin, 2020), and Jon Meacham, *And There Was Light: Abraham Lincoln and the American Struggle* (New York: Random House, 2022). I still find myself going back to David Herbert Donald's great one-volume biography *Lincoln* (New York: Simon & Schuster, 1995). Other biographies worth reading include Richard Carwardine, *Lincoln: A Life of Purpose and Power* (New York: Vintage, 2007), and Ronald C. White Jr., *A. Lincoln: A Biography* (New York: Random House, 2009). Those looking for a more concise biography will find what they are looking for in Mark E. Neely Jr., *The Last Best Hope: Abraham Lincoln and the Promise of America* (Cambridge, MA: Harvard University Press, 1993), and William E. Gienapp, *Abraham Lincoln and Civil War America: A Biography* (New York: Oxford University Press, 2002). The biography that takes the prize for most concise is James M. McPherson, *Abraham Lincoln* (New York: Oxford University Press, 2009), which somehow fits Lincoln's life into seventy-five pages (and small ones at that). Older biographies that used to be the standard fare include Stephen B. Oates, *With Malice Toward None: A Life of Abraham Lincoln* (New York: Harper & Row, 1977), and Benjamin P. Thomas, *Abraham Lincoln* (New York: Knopf, 1952).

Among the many works that focus on Lincoln's presidency are Philip Shaw Paludan, *The Presidency of Abraham Lincoln* (Lawrence: University Press of Kansas, 1994); Doris Kearns Goodwin, *Team of Rivals: The Political Genius of Abraham Lincoln* (New York: Simon & Schuster, 2006); and William Lee Miller, *President Lincoln: The Duty of a Statesman* (New York: Knopf, 2008). The journalist David Von Drehle focuses on the pivotal year of 1862 in *Rise to Greatness: Abraham Lincoln and America's Most Perilous Year* (New York: Holt, 2012). An innovative look at Lincoln's presidential years is provided in Matthew Pinsker, *Lincoln's Sanctuary: Abraham Lincoln and the Soldier's Home* (New York: Oxford University Press, 2005). Also important in understanding Lincoln's wartime leadership is John Fabian Witt's magisterial *Lincoln's Code: The Laws of War in American History* (New York: Free Press, 2012).

No bibliography of Lincoln scholarship, particularly related to Lincoln the politician, would be complete without mention of two older but influential collections: Richard N. Current, *The Lincoln Nobody Knows* (New York: McGraw-Hill, 1956), especially his chapters on "The Master Politician" and "The Most Shut-Mouthed Man"; and David Herbert Donald, *Lincoln Reconsidered: Essays on the Civil War*, 2nd ed. (New York: Vintage, 1961; first published 1956), which includes the must-read essay "A. Lincoln, Politician" as well as the influential if flawed "A Whig in the White House." Another seminal, older essay that cannot go without mention because it is a foil for so much that is written about the Emancipation Proclamation is Richard Hofstadter's brilliant, if ultimately wrongheaded, chapter on "Abraham Lincoln and the Self-Made Myth," in *The American Political Tradition and the Men Who Made It* (New York: Random House, 1948). A collection of some of the best essays on Lincoln, including Current's "Master Politician," is *The Best American History Essays on Lincoln*, ed. Sean Wilentz (New York: Palgrave Macmillan, 2009).

On the relationship between the abolitionists and Lincoln, see James M. McPherson, *The Struggle for Equality: Abolitionists and the Negro in the Civil War and Reconstruction* (Princeton, NJ: Princeton University Press, 1964); Sean Wilentz, *The Politicians and the Egalitarians: The Hidden History of American Politics* (New York: W. W. Norton, 2017), chapter 7 ("Abraham Lincoln: Egalitarian Politician"); and Sidney M. Milkis and Daniel J. Tichenor, *Rivalry and Reform: Presidents, Social Movements, and the Transformation of American Politics* (Chicago: University of Chicago Press, 2019), chapter 2 ("The Crucible: Lincoln and the Abolitionist Movement"). Lincoln's relationship with Frederick Douglass is the focus of two excellent books: James Oakes, *The Radical and the Republican: Frederick Douglass, Abraham Lincoln, and the Triumph of Antislavery Politics* (New York: W. W. Norton, 2007), and John Stauffer, *Giants: The Parallel Lives of Frederick Douglass and Abraham Lincoln* (New York: Twelve, 2008). Lincoln's relationship with Owen Lovejoy is the focus of William F. Moore and Jane Ann Moore, *Collaborators for Emancipation: Abraham Lincoln and Owen Lovejoy* (Urbana: University of Illinois Press, 2014). On Lincoln's relationship with the so-called Radical Republicans in Congress, see Hans L. Trefousse, *The Radical Republicans: Lincoln's Vanguard for Racial Justice* (New York: Knopf, 1969), and Bruce Tap, *Over Lincoln's Shoulder: The Committee on the Conduct of the War* (Lawrence: University Press of Kansas, 1998). Congress's role in ending slavery is emphasized (and Lincoln reduced almost to a spectator) in Fergus Bordewich, *Congress at War: How Republican Reformers Fought the Civil War, Defied Lincoln, Ended Slavery and Remade America* (New York: Knopf, 2020). The Confiscation Acts receive book-length treatment in John Syrett, *The Civil War Confiscation Acts: Failing to Reconstruct the South* (New York: Fordham University Press, 2005). Lincoln's relationship with George McClellan is examined afresh in George C. Rable, *Conflict of Command: George McClellan, Abraham Lincoln, and the Politics of War* (Baton Rouge: Louisiana State University Press, 2023). On Lincoln's relationship with Roger Taney and the Supreme Court, see Brian McGinty, *Lincoln and the Court* (Cambridge, MA: Harvard University Press, 2008), and James F. Simon, *Lincoln and Chief Justice Taney: Slavery, Secession, and the President' War Powers* (New York: Simon & Schuster, 2006).

For those desiring a deeper dive into the Lincoln literature, useful bibliographic essays guiding readers through the cornucopia of writing about Lincoln can be found, among other places, in Paludan, *The Presidency of Abraham Lincoln*; Allen C. Guelzo, *Abraham Lincoln: Redeemer President* (Grand Rapids, MI: William B. Eerdmans, 1999), the second edition of which (published in 2022) includes a new preface that essentially functions as an update to the "Note on the Sources" from the first edition; Ronald C. White Jr., *The Eloquent President: A Portrait of Lincoln through His Words* (New York: Random House, 2005); McPherson, *Abraham Lincoln*; and Michael Holt, *The Election of 1860: "A Campaign Fraught with Consequences"* (Lawrence: University Press of Kansas, 2017). Also still useful is the older historiographical essay in Gabor S. Boritt, *Lincoln and the Economics of the American Dream* (Memphis, TN: Memphis State University Press, 1978).

While the secondary literature on Lincoln is immensely rich, there is no substitute for throwing oneself into primary documents. The main collection of Lincoln's papers, totaling some twenty-thousand documents, much of which is incoming correspondence, are housed in the Library of Congress (https://www.loc.gov/collections/abraham-lincoln-papers/about-this-collection/). Long gone are the days when one had to view these papers on microfilm. Not only are they available on the Library of Congress website but they have been transcribed so that the reader no longer has to decipher nineteenth-century handwriting. Lincoln's own letters, speeches, and other writings have long been available in Roy P. Basler, ed., *The Collected Works of Abraham Lincoln* (New Brunswick, NJ: Rutgers University Press, 1953), which was supplemented with additional material in a volume published in 1974. Those looking for more selective collections of Lincoln's writings have their pick of several fine offerings, including Don E. Fehrenbacher, ed., *Abraham Lincoln: Selected Writings*, 2 vols. (New York: Library of America, 1989); Mario N. Cuomo and Harold Holzer, eds., *Lincoln on Democracy* (New York: HarperCollins, 1990); Andrew Delbanco, ed., *The Portable Abraham Lincoln* (New York: Viking Penguin, 1992); William E. Gienapp, ed., *This Fiery Trial: The Speeches and Writings of Abraham Lincoln* (New York: Oxford University Press, 2012); and David S. Reynolds, ed., *Lincoln's Selected Writings* (New York: W. W. Norton, 2014), which also includes, as do all Norton Critical Editions, a selection of scholarly commentaries on their subject. A wonderful coffee-table book is the beautifully put together and illustrated collection of Lincoln's writings edited by Harold Holzer and Thomas A. Horrocks, *The Annotated Lincoln* (Cambridge, MA: Harvard University Press, 2016).

The writings of Lincoln's private secretaries are a particularly rich source of insight into Lincoln and his decision-making. Michael Burlingame has edited a number of books that have made these diaries, letters, and other writings accessible, the most important of which are Michael Burlingame and John R. Turner Ettlinger, eds., *Inside Lincoln's White House: The Complete Civil War Diary of John Hay* (Carbondale: Southern Illinois University Press, 1997); Michael Burlingame, ed., *With Lincoln in the White House: Letters, Memoranda, and Other Writings of John G. Nicolay, 1860–1865* (Carbondale: Southern Illinois University Press, 2000); and William O. Stoddard, *Inside the White House in War Times: Memoirs and Reports of Lincoln's Secretary*, ed. Michael Burlingame (Lincoln: University of Nebraska Press, 2000). Also instructive is Michael Burlingame, ed., *Lincoln's Journalist: John Hay's Anonymous Writings for the Press, 1860–1864* (Carbondale: Southern Illinois University Press, 1998). Lincoln's private secretaries are the subject of Daniel Mark Epstein, *Lincoln's Men: The President and His Private Secretaries* (New York: HarperCollins, 2009), and the final chapter of David Herbert Donald, *"We Are Lincoln Men": Abraham Lincoln and His Friends* (New York: Simon & Schuster, 2003).

Also important in understanding Lincoln's decision-making related to the proclamation are the diaries and letters of some cabinet members and key members of Congress. Essential is the detailed diary kept by Secretary of the Navy Gideon Welles, the definitive edition of which is William E. Gienapp and Erica L. Gienapp, eds., *The Civil War Diary of Gideon Welles, Lincoln's Secretary of the Navy* (Urbana: University of Illinois Press, 2014). For the diary of Treasury Secretary Salmon Chase, see David Donald, ed., *Inside Lincoln's Cabinet: The Civil War Diaries of Salmon P. Chase* (New York: Longmans, 1954); also see volume 3 (Correspondence, 1858–March 1863) of John Niven, ed., *The Salmon P. Chase Papers* (Kent, OH: Kent State University Press, 1996). Also vital in providing a window into Lincoln's thinking is Theodore Calvin Pease and James G. Randall, eds., *The Diary of Orville Hickman Browning* (Springfield: Illinois State Historical Library, 1925). Useful, too, is Beverly Wilson Palmer, ed., *The Selected Letters of Charles Sumner* (Boston: Northeastern University Press, 1990). For the proclamation specifically, historians have also often drawn from Lincoln's account given to Francis Carpenter, whose iconic painting of Lincoln's first reading of the Emancipation Proclamation to his cabinet hangs today in the United States Capitol. See Francis Carpenter, *The Inner Life of Abraham Lincoln: Six Months at the White House* (Lincoln: University of Nebraska Press, 1985). Many of the recollected words of Lincoln have been collected in Don E. Fehrenbacher and Virginia Fehrenbacher, eds., *Recollected Words of Abraham Lincoln* (Stanford, CA: Stanford University Press, 1996), which opens with a valuable caution against the uncritical use of such recollections. In a related vein, see Douglas L. Wilson and Rodney O. Davis, eds., *Herndon's Informants: Letters, Interviews, and Statements about Abraham Lincoln* (Urbana: University of Illinois Press, 1998).

Although Lincoln is the subject of this book, its starting point is the seminal work of Richard E. Neustadt, *Presidential Power: The Politics of Leadership* (New York: Wiley, 1960). So much work on the American presidency has been written under the influence of Neustadt's monograph that it is not feasible to trace that impact here. However, the interested reader might start by consulting Matthew J. Dickinson and Elizabeth A. Neustadt, eds., *Guardian of the Presidency: The Legacy of Richard E. Neustadt* (Washington, DC: Brookings Institution, 2007), which includes a foreword by his former student, Doris Kearns Goodwin; and Michael Nelson, "Neustadt's 'Presidential Power' at 50," *Chronicle of Higher Education*, March 28, 2010.

Unilateral presidential directives have been the focus of a great deal of study over the past several decades, stimulated in large part by the pioneering work of William G. Howell, particularly his *Power without Persuasion: The Politics of Direct Presidential Action* (Princeton, NJ: Princeton University Press, 2003) and the seminal article that preceded the book, which he wrote with Terry Moe, "The Presidential Power of Unilateral Action," *Journal of Law, Economics, and Organization* (April 1999): 132–179. Among the books on the unilateral presidency that have emerged in the wake of Howell's critique of Neustadt, two have been particularly important in informing my thinking about unilateral directives: Dino P. Christenson and Douglas L. Kriner, *The Myth of the*

Imperial Presidency: How Public Opinion Checks the Unilateral Executive (Chicago: University of Chicago Press, 2020), and Andrew Rudalevige, *By Executive Order: Bureaucratic Management and the Limits of Presidential Power* (Princeton, NJ: Princeton University Press, 2021). Both powerfully reassert the Neustadtian premise of presidential weakness and the constraints on presidential power. Other books that focus on the use and development of unilateral executive directives include Kenneth R. Mayer, *With the Stroke of a Pen: Executive Orders and Presidential Power* (Princeton, NJ: Princeton University Press, 2001); Philip J. Cooper, *By Order of the President: The Use and Abuse of Executive Direct Action* (Lawrence: University Press of Kansas, 2002); Graham G. Dodds, *Take Up Your Pen: Unilateral Presidential Directives in American Politics* (Philadelphia: University of Pennsylvania Press, 2013); and Brandon Rottinghaus and Michelle Belco, *The Dual Executive: Presidential Unilateral Power in a Separated and Shared Power System* (Stanford, CA: Stanford University Press, 2016). Also see Richard J. Ellis, *The Development of the American Presidency*, 4th ed. (New York: Routledge, 2022), chapter 6 ("The Unilateral Presidency: Legislating from the Oval Office").

Nearly ten thousand presidential proclamations, from the first proclamation by George Washington on October 3, 1789, proclaiming a day of Thanksgiving, to the present day, can be found at the invaluable website of the American Presidency Project at the University of California, Santa Barbara: https://www.presidency.ucsb.edu/documents/app-categories/written-presidential-orders/presidential/proclamations. Other types of unilateral directives, notably executive orders and memoranda, can also be found among the voluminous collections of documents housed at the American Presidency Project website.

Central to thinking about the limits on presidential persuasion is the work of George C. Edwards III, particularly his *On Deaf Ears: The Limits of the Bully Pulpit* (New Haven, CT: Yale University Press, 2003). Other works in which Edwards elaborates on the limits of presidential persuasion include *Strategic President: Persuasion and Opportunity in Presidential Leadership* (Princeton, NJ: Princeton University Press, 2009); *Predicting the Presidency: The Potential of Persuasive Leadership* (Princeton, NJ: Princeton University Press, 2016); and *Changing Their Minds? Donald Trump and Presidential Leadership* (Chicago: University of Chicago Press, 2021). Edwards's challenge to the study of presidential rhetoric was forcefully articulated in "Presidential Rhetoric: What Difference Does It Make?," which appeared in Martin J. Medhurst, ed., *Beyond the Rhetorical Presidency* (College Station: Texas A&M University Press, 1996). Among the works critiqued in that essay was David Zarefsky's *Lincoln, Douglas, and Slavery in the Crucible of Public Debate* (Chicago: University of Chicago Press, 1990). Zaresky's riposte can be found in his article "Presidential Rhetoric and the Power of Definition," *Presidential Studies Quarterly* (September 2004): 607–619. Other works exploring the power and limits of presidential rhetoric as well as the causal relationship between presidential action and public opinion include B. Dan Wood, *The Politics of Economic Leadership: The Causes and Consequences of Presidential Rhetoric* (Princeton, NJ: Princeton University Press, 2007); B. Dan Wood, *The Myth of Presidential Representation* (New York: Cambridge University Press, 2009); Jeffrey E. Cohen, *Presidential Responsiveness and Public-Policy Making* (Ann Arbor: University of Michigan Press, 1997); Brandice Canes-Wrone, *Who Leads Whom? Presidents, Policy, and the Public* (Chicago: University of Chicago Press, 2006); Brandon Rottinghaus, *The Provisional Public: Modern Presidential Leadership of Public Opinion* (College Station: Texas A&M University Press, 2010); and Matthew Eshbaugh-Soha and Jeffrey S. Peake, *Breaking through the Noise* (Stanford, CA: Stanford University Press, 2011).

Among the small number of political scientists who have tackled Lincoln's leadership directly is Fred I. Greenstein, who treats Lincoln in a brief final chapter ("Abraham Lincoln: Consummate Leader") of his final book, *Presidents and the Dissolution of the Union: Leadership Style from Polk to Lincoln* (Princeton, NJ: Princeton University Press, 2013). The analysis in that chapter is informed by the categories he first developed in *The Presidential Difference: Leadership Style from FDR to Clinton* (New York: Free Press, 2000).

INDEX

abolitionists
  on Emancipation Proclamation, 5, 50, 82, 83, 91, 122n28, 128n37
  on Frémont's order, 7, 9
  Lincoln and, 23, 29, 82, 92, 95, 118n20, 122n28, 128n37, 129n5
  on Lincoln's leadership, 15, 39, 48, 50, 67, 91, 92, 119n30, 130–131n29
American Colonization Society, 38
American Revolution, 9–10
annual message to Congress
  Lincoln's first, 20, 23, 33–34
  Lincoln's second, 61–68, 75–76
  transmission of, 61
Arkansas, 77, 98
Army of the Potomac, 23, 51, 52. *See also* Union Army
Army of Virginia, 42. *See also* Union Army
Arnold, Isaac, 25–26, 118n21
Aspinwall, William, 52

Bartlett, D. W., 122n28
Bates, Edward, 8, 31, 33, 42, 74, 76, 78, 97
Battle of Antietam, 43–44
Battle of Fredericksburg, 70
Battle of Gettysburg, 86
Battle of Shiloh, 23
Beecher Stowe, Harriet, 125n9
Bell, John, 48

Bennett, Leonard, 95
Benton, Thomas Hart, 7
Blacks
  as agents of recruitment, 91
  Dred Scott case and, 97
  employment of, 63–64, 73–74, 126–127n18
  Lincoln's attempts to persuade, 36–39
  military enlistment of, 73–74, 85–86, 88–89, 97, 98–99
  northward migration of, 56–57, 64
  White racism toward, 21, 33, 35, 56, 57, 58, 123n11
Blair, Frank, 7–8, 14, 21–22
Blair, Montgomery, 7–8, 14, 31, 45–46, 76, 78
border states
  Black military service and, 74
  colonization and, 33–34
  compensated emancipation and, 19–27, 66
  concerns of, 28–29
  desertion in, 40, 84
  elections in, 59
  Emancipation Proclamation effects on, 46, 98
  gradual emancipation and, 46, 96
  Lincoln's appeal to, 23–24
  political support from, 18, 98
  secession and, 46
  See also specific states

Britain, emancipation decrees of, 9–10
Brown, John, 116n4
Browning, Orville, 16–17, 20, 29, 55, 65, 71, 105n15, 122n24
Buchanan, James, 16
Burlingame, Michael, 15, 66, 115n14
Burton, Benjmain, 19–20
Bush, George W., 103n11
Butler, General Benjamin, 10–11

Cameron, Simon, 10–11, 15
Camp Nelson, 85
Carpenter, Francis, 82
Casey, Samuel, 125–126n10
Central America, colonization plan regarding, 36, 38, 108n2
Central High School (Little Rock, Arkansas), 2, 3
Chase, Salmon
    on Emancipation Proclamation, 31, 37, 47, 73, 76–77, 112n11, 126n15, 126n16
    on Frémont's emancipation order, 9
    on Lincoln's rescinding of Frémont's order, 16
    Lincoln's outmaneuvering of, 71
    on Republican elections, 54
    on Restored Government of Virginia, 78
    warns Lincoln about unrealistic plan, 67
Chicago Tribune (newspaper), 38, 45
Chiriquí project, 34, 36, 38, 44

Christenson, Dino, 3, 97, 103n11
Civil War
    Battle of Antietam in, 43–44
    Battle of Gettysburg in, 86
    Battle of Shiloh in, 23
    desertion in, 84
    purpose of, 11, 26, 47, 87, 118n26
    Second Battle of Bull Run in, 42
    Siege of Vicksburg in, 86
Clay, Henry, 38
Cleveland, Grover, 1
colonization plan, 33–39, 48–49, 63–64, 108n2, 109–110n16, 113n4, 114–115n14
command
    cost of, 3, 13, 15, 60
    as last resort, 2–3, 4, 83
    limits of 1–4, 5, 83, 86, 98, 100–101
    commander in chief, 25, 31, 41, 47, 72, 87, 110n27
compensated emancipation, 19–27, 62–63, 65, 108n2, 109n16. *See also* emancipation
Confederate Army, 42, 51, 86–87
Confiscation Act. *See* First Confiscation Act; Second Confiscation Act
Confiscation-Emancipation Act. *See* Second Confiscation Act
Congress
    annual message to, 61
    compensated emancipation and, 20–21, 27
    constitutional power of, 29
    emancipation policy support from, 71

Militia Act and, 73–74, 97
Restored Government of
Virginia and, 78
congressional elections, 50–60,
76, 120n9, 127n9
constitutional racism, 123n11
Conway, Moncure, 15, 92, 118n20,
124–125n1
Copperheads, 85
Creswell, John, 132n11
Crisfield, John, 22
Cutler, William P., 65

Davis, David, 62, 66
Davis, Garrett, 34, 109n16
Davis, Jefferson, 99
Dawes, Henry, 65, 70
Delaware, 19, 20, 55, 66, 98,
108n2
Democratic Party, 1, 18, 23, 46,
50–60, 72
Department of the West, 8
desegregation, 2, 3
desertion, 84
Dickson, William, 125n5
District of Columbia,
emancipation in, 34, 64,
109n16
Doolittle, James, 109n16
Douglas, Stephen, 55
Douglass, Frederick, 37, 38, 65,
90–92, 93, 119n30
Dred Scott case, 97

Edwards, George, 2–3
Eisenhower, Dwight, 1, 2, 3
elections, 50–60
emancipation

compensated, 19–27, 62–63, 65,
108n2, 109n16
concerns regarding, 64
Frémont's proclamation of, 7–9
gradual, 20, 21, 78–79
Hunter's decree of, 23, 25
importance of, 49
Lincoln's decision for, 28–32
Lincoln's reply to Greeley on,
33, 47–49
military, 69, 93
as military necessity, 30, 49, 57,
58, 72–73, 88, 128n37
paradox of, 93
public support for, 118n20
self-, 75
Emancipation Memorial, 39
Emancipation Proclamation
as act of justice, 72–73, 97,
126n16
authority invoked by Lincoln
in, 31, 47, 72
cabinet discussions of, 31–32
43–47, 72–73
criticisms of, 52–53, 55, 84, 87
effects of, 93–94
effects on Union Army, 84
electoral effects of, 53–60
exemptions in, 76–77
final version of, 72–80, 127n22,
130n18
implementation challenges of,
83–86, 90–94
as last card, 4, 43, 96, 112–
113n15
as last resort, 4, 83, 96, 101
legal concerns and, 18, 66, 73,
79, 107n40, 130n18

Emancipation Proclamation, *continued*
  lessons and legacies of, 95–101
  limitations of, 97–98
  Lincoln's concerns regarding, 40, 41–42, 97
  Lincoln's expectations for, 82–83, 129n5
  Lincoln's goals regarding, 40–41, 72–73, 87–88, 130n22
  Lincoln's public defense of, 87–89
  military necessity and, 30, 72–73, 88, 126n16, 128n37
  McClellan's reaction to, 52–53
  preliminary, 40–49
  public response to, 47–48, 49, 50–51, 83, 97, 128n1
  public's readiness for, 117–118n20
  revisions to final version of, 73–76, 126n16, 127n22, 130n18
  significance of, 81–83
  signing of, 79
  Sumner's influence on wording of, 72–73, 126n16
  timing of, 32, 43–44, 59, 97, 100, 118n25
England, 99
Ewing, Thomas, 111n4

Fessenden, Samuel, 71
Fessenden, William Pitt, 16, 71
First Confiscation Act
  conditions of, 11–12, 15
  debates regarding, 118–119n26
  Lincoln's actions regarding, 17
  Lincoln's view of, 29, 111n4
  Second Confiscation Act compared to, 28
Fisher, George P., 19, 20–21, 55, 111n29
Florida, 23, 77
Foner, Eric, 37–38, 77, 100
Forbes, John Murray, 72, 73, 126n13
Fortress Monroe, 10
France, 99
Frémont, Jessie, 12, 14, 106n27
Frémont, John C.
  emancipation order of, 9, 11
  leadership style of, 14
  letter to Lincoln from, 13–14
  Lincoln's attempt to persuade, 11–12, 13–14, 16–17
  overview of, 7–9
Fugitive Slave Law of 1850, 10–11

Gamble, Hamilton, 8, 124n16
Garibaldi, Giuseppe, 81
Garnet, Henry Highland, 83
Garrison, William Lloyd, 15, 128n1
Gay, Sydney, 48
Georgia, 23
Gettysburg Address, 4–5
gradual emancipation, 20, 21, 78–79. *See also* emancipation
Grant, Ulysses, 85–86
grapevine telegraph, 91
Greeley, Horace, 33, 41, 45, 47–48, 57, 108n2, 119n27, 125n1
Grimes, Joseph, 7
Grow, Galusha, 54
Guelzo, Allen, 54, 59, 65, 130n18

Haiti, 76
Hale, John, 124n16
Halleck, Henry, 86
Hamlin, Hannibal, 51
Hay, John, 75, 96, 105n15
Henderson, John, 48, 124n16
Hofstadter, Richard, 81–82, 95
Holt, Joseph, 107n31
House of Representatives. *See* Congress
Hunter, General David, 14, 23, 25, 110n27

Illinois, 55, 56–57
Inaugural Address, Lincoln's, 5
Indiana, 54
isothermalism, 123n11

Jackson, Claiborne, 8, 9, 104n6
Johnson, Andrew, 77
Johnson, Reverdy, 113n15

Kennedy, John F., 1
Kentucky, 12–13, 20, 59, 66, 98, 105n17
Key, John J., 51–52
Kock, Bernard, 76
Kriner, Douglas, 3, 97, 103n11

Lee, Robert E., 42, 44, 45, 53, 86, 93
Lester, Julius, 5
Liberator (newspaper), 15
Lincoln, Abraham
  annual messages of, 20, 23, 33–34, 61–68, 75–76
  appeal to border states by, 23–24, 26
  authority claimed by, 17, 18, 31, 47, 72, 88, 110n27
  colonization advocated by, 20, 25, 33–39, 44–45, 63, 64–65, 67, 75–76, 96, 100, 109n16, 114–115n14
  commander in chief clause invoked by, 31, 47, 72, 110n27
  covenant with God invoked by, 44–45, 46, 79
  criticism of, 5, 15–16, 18, 30, 37, 43, 48, 60, 65, 70, 92, 95, 100, 106n27
  on Emancipation Proclamation's significance, 82–83
  emotions of, 29, 42, 49, 51, 59, 69, 71
  failure to persuade by, 13, 19–27, 31, 33–39
  on God's purposes, 41
  Inaugural Address of, 5
  loss of political mastery by, 43
  popularity of, 60, 70, 90
  on presidential power, 18, 30, 100–101
  professional reputation of, 60, 67
  reply to Greeley by, 33, 47–48
  on signing of the Emancipation Proclamation, 79
  on slavery, 17–18, 33, 41, 62, 67, 74, 105n15
  virtue of, 100–101
  way with words, 4–5
  weakness of, 5, 32, 43, 49, 60, 96, 97
Lincoln, Mary Todd, 79

Little Rock, Arkansas, 2, 3
Livermore, George, 126n16
Louisiana, 77, 98, 108n2
Lovejoy, Owen, 21, 25–26
Lyon, Nathaniel, 9, 104n9

MacArthur, General Douglas, 2, 3
Maine, 54
March to the Sea, 93
Marx, Karl, 50
Maryland, 12, 20, 22, 34, 59, 66, 98, 132n11
Masur, Kate, 113n4
McClellan, General George, 23, 30, 42–44, 51–53
McClintock, John, 117–118n20
Medill, Joseph, 16
"Memorial of all Christian Denominations," 40
military emancipation, 9–10. *See also* emancipation
Militia Act, 73–74, 97
Mississippi, 77
Missouri, 7, 8–9, 12, 20, 22, 66, 124n16
Mitchell, James, 34, 113n4, 114n14
Morton, Oliver, 54
Mott, Lucretia, 9

National Anti-Slavery Standard (newspaper), 15
National Intelligencer (newspaper), 48
Neely, Mark, 39, 43, 48, 100, 119n27
Neustadt, Richard, xi–xiii, 1–4, 5, 39, 49, 83, 96, 98, 103n4
New Jersey, 55–56

New York, 55–56, 57–58
New York Tribune (newspaper), 33, 45, 72–73, 108n2, 125n1
New York World (newspaper), 105n15
Niagara Manifesto, 131n31
Nicolay, John, 30, 54, 61
Noell, John, 22
North Carolina, 77

Oakes, James
  on Civil War, 85, 86, 93
  on Emancipation Proclamation, 49, 75, 96, 98, 99, 117n20, 118n20
  on Second Confiscation Act, 28
Obama, Barack, 103n11
Ohio, 54, 58, 90
Oregon, 53, 54
Owen, Robert Dale, 49

Pelletan, Eugène, 95
Peninsular Campaign, 23, 30, 42
Pennsylvania, 54, 58, 90
persuasion, power of, 1–3, 5, 18, 86, 101
Philadelphia Press (newspaper), 50
Phillips, Wendell, 48, 92, 98, 105n15, 118n20, 122n28, 129n5
Polk, James, 1
Pomeroy, Samuel, 38, 114–115n14
Pope, General John, 42
power
  limitations on, 1–2, 49, 98
  of persuasion, 1, 2–3, 101
  to resist, 3, 39

powers
  of command, 30, 98
  of commander in chief, 25, 31, 41, 47, 72, 110n27
  contrasted with power, 1, 49, 53
  "The Prayer of Twenty Millions" (Greeley), 33, 45
presidential power
  limits of, 2, 79
  Lincoln's understanding of, 18, 30, 100–101
  Neustadt's understanding of, 1–3, 49, 103n4
  persuasion and, 1–3, 101
  unilateralism and, 3–4
  unrealistic expectations of, 95, 101
Presidential Power (Neustadt), xi, 1–2, 103n4
presidential weakness, 2, 3, 5, 32, 43, 49, 60, 96, 97, 142
professional reputation, 60, 67

Quincy, Edmund, 15

racism, 21, 35, 123n11
Raymond, Henry, 90
Republican Party
  divisions within, 58, 122n24
  elections and, 50–60, 90, 93–94
  Emancipation Proclamation and, 89, 100
  slavery and, 17
Restored Government of Virginia, 77–78
Richmond, Virginia, 23
Rudalevige, Andrew, 80

Schurz, Carl, 56
Scott, General Winfield, 106–107n29
Scripps, John L., 16
Second Battle of Bull Run, 42
Second Confiscation Act
  conditions of, 31, 41–42, 47, 126–127n18
  Congressional action regarding, 76, 96
  First Confiscation Act as compared to, 28
  'forever free' language in, 28, 130n18
  Lincoln and, 28, 29–30, 32, 45
  Section 6, 31
  Section 9, 28
  Section 11, 28, 126–127n18
  Section 12, 28
  Seymour's criticism of, 56
Senate. *See* Congress
Seward, William Henry, 29, 43, 44, 45, 70–71, 75, 76, 78
Seymour, Horatio, 55–56, 57
Sherman, General William Tecumseh, 93
Sherman, John, 29, 54, 118–119n26
Siege of Vicksburg, 86
slavery
  Lincoln's view of, 17–18, 33, 41, 62, 67, 74, 105n15
  self-emancipation from, 75
  statistics regarding, 93, 105n17, 123n4
  vastness of, 93
South Carolina, 23, 77
Speed, James, 112n14
Speed, Joshua, 12, 112n14

Springfield, Missouri, 9
Stanton, Edwin, 29, 56–57, 78, 92, 111n4
State of the Union. *See* annual message to Congress
steel industry, 2, 3
Stevens, Thaddeus, 119n26
St. Louis, Missouri, 8, 9
Stowe, Harriet Beecher, 125n9
Strong, George Templeton, 70, 125n9
Stuart, J. E. B., 56
Sumner, Charles, 15, 18, 20, 66, 69, 123n4, 125n9, 126n16
Swett, Leonard, 55, 57
systemic racism, 35

Tennessee, 12, 77, 98, 105n17
Thirteenth Amendment, 99
Thomas, Benjamin, 70
Thomas, Edward M., 114n11
Thomas, Lorenzo, 15, 37, 84
Tilton, Theodore, 122n28
Truman, Harry, 1, 2, 3
Trump, Donald, 103n11
Tyler, Moses Coit, 81, 128n1

Unconditional Union Party, 59
unilateral directives, 80, 97, 103n11, 116n4, 141–142
unilateral presidency, 95
Union Army, 43–44, 50, 70, 83–84, 85, 86, 93–94
Usher, John P., 34, 113n3

Van Vleet, Jacob, 34–35, 114n11
Virginia, 10, 77, 98

Wadsworth, James, 55–56, 58
War Department, 91
War of 1812, 10
Washington, DC, 42
Weed, Thurlow, 32, 44, 48, 57–58
Welles, Gideon, 27, 30, 42, 46–47, 78, 117n20
West Virginia, 59, 77, 78–79, 98
White, Jonathan, 84
Wickliffe, Charles, 22
Wilson, Douglas L., 119n27, 119n29
Witt, John Fabian, 17
Wood, Fernando, 55
Wright, Elizur, 118n20

www.ingramcontent.com/pod-product-compliance
Lightning Source LLC
Chambersburg PA
CBHW021735220426
43662CB00008B/866